The
That Always Smiles

My Brain Haemorrhage Journey

By

Jo Ulczak

The Mask That Always Smiles -
MY BRAIN HAEMORRHAGE JOURNEY

ISBN: 978-1-0369-0059-5

First published in Great Britain in 2024 through Amazon self-publishing service

Produced by **samanthahoughton.co.uk**

Dedication

I wish to dedicate my book to my parents, who have been there for me every hour of every day throughout my recovery from my brain haemorrhage.

It's not been easy; in fact, it has been extremely exhausting at times. Having enthusiasm, dedication, and motivation every day to help me with my walking, exercises, and daily living is extremely powerful and has never gone unappreciated, even in the most difficult times.

Contents

Prologue xvii

Chapter One: Welcome to my world 1

Chapter Two: My AVM. .17

Chapter Three: Sensations and Post-Bleed Symptoms . .33

Chapter Four: It's All Just a Balancing Act/Recalibrate . .89

Chapter Five: Walk the Line 99

Chapter Six: Acknowledgement 123

Chapter Seven: Not an Overnight Fixture 135

Chapter Eight: You Only Knew a Part of Me... Which No Longer Exists 193

Chapter Nine: The Mask That Always Smiles 203

Chapter Ten: Hard but Not Impossible 211

Chapter Eleven: Don't Forget to Cry (Emotions) 225

Chapter Twelve: Looking Forward. 235

Chapter Thirteen: Patience 245

Thank you 249

Connect With Me. 251

"YOU ARE
Braver than you believe
Stronger than you seem
Smarter than you think
And loved more than you know."

A.A. Milne

People who give you the time of day are worth keeping hold of.

I learned a lot during my recovery time based on my perceptions. Well, I had much time to take in and understand life. It created a greater understanding of myself, which I had never had before.

So, it is said that we all have a story inside us to tell. I searched for mine for years, but it was normal: go to work, eat, sleep, save money, go on holiday, buy nice things, and repeat it all. I hadn't found anything to share with others until now. Only this story is not one I would wish to share, as I would rather not have experienced it. That is, of course, if I looked at the experience with a half-empty glass. When looking at it with a half-full glass, it is knowledge now gained and if I help just one other person, it will be so rewarding.

I know from personal experience how difficult it is to seek out guidance for my situation. I found there was very little on offer. No one had documented a bleed within the brain similar to mine. It seemed through all my research looking for guidance that if a bleed occurred that had to do with the brain, it was usually on the outside of the brain, causing many symptoms which were slightly different to my own. This makes me no hero to be here alive, and I have come to the point of recovery, which I'm at. However, we must stay strong and keep positive that it will all ease up in time.

I've been no book reader since my bleed, and I don't even read magazines. This is no doubt down to my damaged left-eye vision. Why would I want to write a book when I don't even read them? I have no concept of where to start, how to go about one, etc., so I apologise now if you find errors or get confused with my writing. I only know that the last handful of years from having a bleed within the brain, which was just off the brainstem and labelled as "severe" by my neurologist, has concluded in being a rare circumstance only resulting in showing evidence of there being a lack of resources to help one through this situation.

This is when I started to feel I needed to write a book. I needed to document my journey. I wanted to tell others alike that they are not alone. I needed to share my experience in the hope that it would help others. If I take anything away from this situation, it will be knowledge and understanding to share with others. I do not choose to be placed through this hardship and unable to offer anything from it. I had no help, and I had to find my own feet in my own way. No one knew the outcome, and no one had experience with my situation to offer me help. As hard as it was, keeping positive and believing in the recovery proved to be the best medicine.

Yes, it's an extremely hard journey, though it is not impossible. Given plenty of patience, there was a light at the end of the tunnel. I ignored all negative feedback and predictions and continued my home rehabilitation routine. I somehow had stored enthusiasm and determination to win the battle of reaching a platform of independence.

I want my life event to be acknowledged and used as a resource in helping others. When friends and family say they understand what you're going through, they really don't. How could they? How could anyone? I only know this as I have had the privilege of living life without and with a brain injury. The situation is so unique to the individual that others can't understand as they are not living with the symptoms daily.

Writing my account of the incident which you are about to discover has been my therapy throughout my recovery, and I promised myself how I would share my journey, which I have contended over the years. I was not fortunate enough to be handed the cards life dealt me once - I was honoured with a second opportunity. You had to be holding the joker for this to happen. Not that it's a funny journey, just a very unfortunate one. This encouraged me to document my journey throughout my recovery, mainly through bullet points and short paragraphs, as my vision was particularly poor, resulting in my inability to write any actual paragraphs. My fatigue levels were also especially poor, resulting in my inability to spend much time writing notes.

Self-expression was my release and way of articulating my symptoms, feelings, improvements and recovery acknowledgements throughout my recovery time. However, recovery is for life, as you are always improving. I would talk to myself but not in a way that others viewed me as slightly crazy. Still, mentally, I was walking my way through my recovery, making notes of symptoms, remedies and challenging situations which I had encountered. I have included some dated notes taken and diary entries within the chapters of my book. Everyone who encounters a brain injury will experience a different experience with the healing process; it's not one shoe fits all.

Before you dive into a moment of my life and world, always remember that I have centred this journey on my experience and my experience alone. What you will read is only my account and findings regarding my situation. A specialist, medic or doctor has not endorsed it. It will not hold answers for your journey, as it will be very different from mine. Please don't see it as a medical journal. I was fortunate enough to document my journey so that I could share it with others, hoping to help and inspire someone and for them never to lose hope in achieving their goals.

This book will be my account of the immediate post years which I endured through the bleeding in my brain. I wish to offer positivity, determination, and enthusiasm and for you to never give up when finding positive energy is extremely hard.

My book will not be for everyone. Some may find it intense, unattractive, non-interesting, and that, to me, is completely fine. I will not be distressed if you do not wish to read my story. It's a journey that occurs unexpectedly, as it most often happens. I have discovered that no one wakes up to the day knowing the journey ahead will encounter a brain haemorrhage, and maybe that's what makes it most interesting. It's not a journey I wish anyone to encounter, as it is unpleasant. It tests your inner strength to the max. You must keep positive, and wearing a smile every day of the year helps you through, no matter how much you cry. Improvement is slow and is not recognised daily but monthly or even in monthly blocks. You don't register the improvements immediately; it is only over time you notice the improvement, no matter how small. Improvement can be so minor and something we take for granted, like kneeling. I couldn't kneel for over a year, but then this action became more pain-free. I was slowly, over time, being able to kneel again. I struggled to bend my knees as they hurt so much, and I would sway side to side so much that I was unable to balance on my knees. I was completely unstable.

There's a phrase you'll see me use repeatedly throughout my book to describe my bleed, and that is: "within my brain" due to the nature of the type of haemorrhage I experienced.

animal

Prologue

Do I know you?

For the many who know me, you will all know me as the individual I was before my brain bleed. I am now a new version of that individual. The bleed altered my opinions, limitations, and abilities, creating a new version of myself. I am still me, though slightly improved. Some will say I'm quite the opposite. And some will prefer the old me.

I was previously a very active individual. I loved surfing, playing tennis, going on long coastal walks, cycling, meeting up with friends, and being free and independent. I loved going out for a drive by myself or with company, exploring new places, taking photos, and creating memories. I was never really a 'laze-about' but was a get-up-and-go person. I didn't have time for breakfast as I needed to seize the moment. Yes, breakfast is super important, but I sometimes would delay it. After all, the sunrise wouldn't wait for my breakfast. If this resulted in me having to swap my bowl of cereal for a breakfast bar and tub of fruit at my desk later, then this was the sacrifice to enjoy the sunrise moment. After work, I would enjoy either surfing in the refreshing ocean, yes, I say refreshing as it was mostly damned cold, or enjoying a nice coastal walk. I always enjoyed participating in something after work as it completed my day, and I didn't just spend it at work.

I also enjoyed the sunshine, so where I could, I would take holidays in sunny destinations where the surf was good. And if possible, the ocean water was warm - I wasn't asking for much! I visited quite a few locations and am very pleased I did. With my current situation, I can't imagine I will continue to travel the world, as it's quite challenging and exhausting when stripped of your independence.

Throughout my life, I have often been quite unwell. Now, I'm not speaking about having a cold; I'm talking more about the (ME) Myalgic Encephalomyelitis level the doctors diagnosed, which they also refer to as Chronic Fatigue Syndrome (CFS). This long-term condition has many symptoms, though the most common is extreme tiredness. I found it extremely difficult to lift any limb; using my muscles was difficult and painful sometimes. It wouldn't matter how much rest I had incurred; I was still extremely fatigued. This illness would interfere with my schooling quite frequently, and having others understand was quite challenging as, being of school age, others often saw me as trying to dodge the obvious.

I was quite shy and quiet, and upon leaving school, I still contended with this condition as I felt it was a part of who I was. I would have good episodes and bad ones. Along with carrying this burden of a condition, I also suffered from depression, anxiety and constant headaches, which would last days on end; again, the doctor advised me it was all good. The headaches were consistent, and they didn't perform any investigation. I kept quiet to friends regarding the anxiety and depression, though I was on different medications to help ease the symptoms. I also suffered from fevers and a continual unwell left eye, conjunctivitis being its favourite friend. I also contended that my legs and knees were sore while growing up, though the doctors always told me they were growing pains. I struggled with my breathing; this interfered with my sports, though it didn't stop me. My doctor prescribed me an inhaler, though I'm not convinced they helped. I don't think it was asthma. Looking back now and contending with what I do today, I think it linked to what was going on in my brain, as I have mild breathing difficulties since my bleed, so I can only imagine it was another symptom. I can also say this: for my constant headaches, fevers, eye concerns and legs causing me problems; I feel it was all linked. Despite this ill health side to my life, I was always smiling.

My love for the ocean and surfing was in the family as my Dad surfed. I would compete in British-based competitions. This one time, I was participating in a tag team event, which consisted of four surfers who each caught two waves. The team with the highest score won. It was my turn to surf, and upon running down to the water, my legs gave from under me, and I collapsed, and I passed out briefly. It was all short-lived, and when I came around, I bounced back up, laughed, and continued my journey to the sea. Looking at this occurrence now makes me feel it links to what was happening in my brain.

This same incident, but a different scenario, happened to me later in life, and then again, it totalled three episodes. Although I was fit and healthy, something within me was making my legs give out on me, having me collapse to the floor and briefly pass out. It was all very embarrassing then. Who wishes to be watched when falling?

As you will now discover, what happened to me left me with this decision. I have two directions I can choose to follow with what I'm about to share with you. I can go left and tell you how tough and depressing my journey has been, or I can go right and show you all the positives and greatness you can achieve from a bad situation. Well, I'm not going to drown you with bad times and how tough and depressing this journey has been, as it is definitely that, and that goes without saying. Still, saying that I will shed light on the hard times, as it has made me who I am today. So, a huge positive has come from this happening.

You never know how strong you are until being strong is your only choice.

Bob Marley

Chapter One | Welcome to my world

No one really knows of the traumatic time my family and I endured from June 2017 onwards. This was the month and year my life drastically changed. Even though I was saved that day, a part of me died. I was no longer the Jo everyone knew.

No brain bleed is a good thing, though if I was not unfortunate enough to endure this encounter a second time around (yes, it bled twice), I had to have the bleed deep within the brain, within the Cerebellum, to be precise, as opposed to being on the outside of the brain. There's always someone who must be awkward. If it had been on the outside, then it would have been accessible and could have been dealt with quicker and easier. However, that does not guarantee that I would not have concerns and symptoms to contend with, as damage to any area of the brain can cause symptoms. It occurred not far off the brain stem, and I'm told by many that I am very lucky to have survived the occurrence.

It was unfortunate that the cause of my bleeding was a natural creation and was a ticking time bomb just waiting to go off. I had lived with this my entire life and knew nothing of its existence. I could not have the creation removed due to its location, so my only option was to undertake a Gamma Knife procedure, which would result in shrinking the damaged area to zero. No, there was no actual knife involved. The name makes it sound worse than it is, or it makes it sound more exciting than it actually is. However you wish to look at it, it's a precise radio beam which zaps the area of concern with its aim to shrink the damaged area over a handful of years, which is the creation of the bleed. Doctors warn you there is a risk of a re-bleed occurrence while it is shrinking, though I was also informed this is extremely rare; the odds behind this happening were extremely low. I was the lucky winner when I received the rare winner prize.

During my first-year post-bleed, time took a step back. Everything moved that much slower. You see just how fast the world is moving. I was no longer part of the fast lane; it was moving so fast that people were forgetting the importance of living. You see a lot within the temporary period of living with a prominent injury. It's like time really slows down, and you see how much people are rushing about and living with daily stress and anxiety. I was once one of these people.

Each new day felt like the same day symptom-wise for me; deja vu comes to mind. I would go to bed and wake up feeling exactly the same. It's by far soul-destroying, but only if you let it. I had to look at the situation as a challenge, an opportunity to remake myself, only a better version than before. The bleed had taken me back to scratch; I had to rebuild all my muscles, starting with my back and neck muscles so that I could hold myself up right as I was a wobbly mess. I had to rebalance my body, which took not months but years. I couldn't walk without assistance, even at five years post-bleed. My vision was still ongoing with repair five years post-bleed. The positive is that it all started improving with time, though I never reached one hundred per cent. Recovery for me wasn't a matter of days, weeks or months, it was a matter of years. They are not lying when they say you need P&P (not postage and packaging but prayer and patience).

On the outside, you would know nothing different from my troublesome time until I started walking. Then, you may question whether there is something up.

No one really understands what you must contend with daily, not even another survivor, as we are all so unique, and our bodies accept the injury differently and, therefore, heal differently. Everyone experiences a different journey. All injuries to the brain are serious no matter who you are, how small or big it appears to be or how you acquired it.

People will insist they understand, though, in all honesty, they know nothing of your journey and have no insight into your daily demons. They may spend every hour of every day with you, but they will never understand the troubles you are contending with.

If anyone ever asks how I can write a book on a brain haemorrhage, I would simply reply there is so much involved that no one would understand or comprehend. I can make this assumption boldly.

As I have previously stated, there was very little help and support for my bleeding within the brain. Trust me, I know. Forums were my best friend. People who had experienced similar circumstances and symptoms had the best advice. I did encounter individuals on forums who were extremely helpful, and I also encountered individuals who were quite the opposite. That is to be expected, as not everyone will accept that you may be worse off than they are.

As time passed, I became less inclined to write an account of my experience. The demons started entering my thoughts in a manner, asking and taunting me about what makes my story and journey any more exciting than someone else's, words which I would repeat to myself? Why would someone wish to read my story? I had to see through these negative thoughts and act accordingly upon them. I would think that if we acted upon these thoughts, it would conclude in doing nothing every time. I feel many individuals don't make themselves known as they feel no one will be interested in their story, or they will be judged or labelled as having a brain injury or simply not giving the individual the time of day. Only these individuals hold most of the information that is valuable to others. They just don't realise it.

My answer to many questions was always that my journey is my journey only. I wish to support others who have been handed a hard path to follow, especially with their health. I want to share how I changed my mindset even though I believe I cried on the inside every day for over three years.

Thankfully, I couldn't produce actual tears, so no one saw my pain. It was a case of 'Jo looks fine, so she must be fine.' Little would they know, I had poor balance, was unable to walk unaided or far, internally swayed, had poor vision, limited taste, my left leg felt like how I imagined Meccano to feel, my right calf muscle itched to explode, there were bouncing brain sensations, and the list goes on... I will stop there as it's starting to get boring.

It was turning into, 'I talk the talk,' but was I going to 'walk the walk'? Due to the lack of specialist support I received; I made it a top priority to see this book written.

It became quite easy for me to get into the state of mind that it's been a long time since this all began, and I'm still not getting my independence. But on the flip side, as hard as it was to see, I was always that bit closer to achieving it.

I had favourite words during my recovery. These included evident, prominent, conclusive, obvious and apparent. Everything was black and white; if there was a reason behind the answer, then the answer was obvious. I noticed that we as humans were very good at avoiding the answer, so instead, we would change how we represent the answer so as not to make ourselves look opinionated even if the answer is super obvious. Now, being the way I was temporarily programmed, I would see this obvious avoidance and state the clear as-day answer. This would no doubt go against me on occasions in that individuals would think, "I can't believe Jo just said that, etc", though what would I honestly care? I can't paint a pretty picture when there's not one to be painted.

From what I have researched, every brain injury is so different. What works for one person may not work for another. This leaves us with very little evidence for advice and guidance, which is beyond frustrating as this is the one thing the injured craves. We want to get better and want to know how. But it's that usual story of how no one can see the damage - we don't know how to treat it. If it were visual, then the best approach would be able to be calculated, but in a brain injury case, we simply don't know.

The bleed altered my emotions slightly. I became emotionless. It was like whatever emotion cells I had were now gone. In one sense, it was good as it kept the tears and depression away, but in another, it was a case of I either liked you or I didn't. There was no middle ground; it was either yes or no, whatever the topic of conversation would be.

The year 2018 was a complete struggle for the entire three hundred and sixty-five days. I started the year being wheel chaired everywhere, which the medics then replaced with walking aids, which resulted in being more of a hindrance than a help. After that, I was link-armed and assisted everywhere. My brain hadn't settled enough for me to venture anywhere alone. However, attempting it wouldn't have worked for me as I couldn't walk without physical assistance. I also couldn't see clearly, as everything was out of focus. I had no perspective on my vision, meaning I couldn't judge any depths; everything was 2D. My energy levels were also non-existent, stemming mainly from the brain. Because it had to work so hard, it tired out super quickly. There was brain fatigue, which I had never experienced before, making it a struggle to walk a few steps assisted. The saying, *"You don't know how strong you are until being strong is your only option,"* kept me going through this troublesome time.

Positive vibes are a winner for anyone. Especially when you're in a pretty unfortunate position. Being fortunate enough to be around this type of person will bring you forward leaps and bounds. If you can portray this attribute yourself then you are a strong individual and in my eyes being positive is seen as a top medicine for recovery. If you can put aside all demons to carry out your day, no matter how challenging, then that must be rewarding. Sometimes, you must remind yourself of these achievements as you can easily overlook them. Achievement can be tiny, but we must remind ourselves that achievement is achievement, no matter how small it may be.

For me, it wasn't a case of not putting the effort and repetition in on movements, it was the actual brain being the alpha male. If my brain didn't allow me to perform the movements, you could see it as a waste of time. I enjoyed practising actions as it gave me something to do and focus on; it kept me active and stimulated, so I kept at it. It wasn't easy, and it was super disheartening at times. It was humiliating and embarrassing; after all, I had lived thirty-six years being able to do these simple tasks. I think this was where some of my motivation stemmed from. The idea was that all was once possible, so why should it be any different now? It took a while to accept that I would no doubt perform the tasks/movements slightly differently, though I had to remind myself that by looking at the situation positively, I could still perform these tasks. It took around two years to achieve this mindset, so this is the time it took for the brain to start settling. Even at four and half year's post-bleed, I still struggled with confidence towards my new approach to my daily living. I had improved, though we always want to be more advanced.

I remember being thirty months forward from the day of the bleed and still struggling to walk independently, as I am to this day, to see correctly, to balance, and to carry out my daily exercises unassisted. It was super hard and draining. I would use so much energy to try to see correctly that it would leave me with little energy to carry out my tasks. I believed it was improving, though this was happening at a very slow pace.

I felt as though the situation within my brain was settling, but I had to hold onto this thought and believe in it. No one could advise on the situation as they could not see it to comment.

I would practice going up steps/stairs without using a handrail for assistance nearly every day. At around three years post-bleed, I could manage three steps going up unassisted well without the handrail. However, I achieved them with over-exaggerated wide steps for balance. I really needed a handrail. I would practice most days as I thought if I was stranded with steps and no handrail on offer, how would I escape? It was this thought that pushed me to achieve the goal of moving up and down steps unassisted. I was still practising five-plus years later to achieve this for a handful of steps confidently. But I did achieve it. I may be achieving this outcome with a new approach but remembering that I was unable to practice this during the first eighteen months after the bleed due to my continual shaking and super poor balance, I found it quite rewarding.

I also practised putting on any bottoms whilst standing unaided after the first two years, be it shorts/trousers/skirt, etc., to strengthen my balance. I had the same chain of thought of being stranded with nothing to hold or lean on; how would I manage? It was the being stranded frame of mind which pushed me to practice. I didn't want to be the one who couldn't get away due to limited capabilities.

I would teach myself new ways to achieve the outcome I wanted. This new me was the same person who now achieved activities differently. My love for long walks, especially if there was a nice coastline involved, was an activity I could no longer perform, so I replaced it with a supported visit to the gym a couple of times a week. I had to be taken and supported due to my capabilities. I was never a gym goer before my bleed, but it was now the easiest way to exercise and feel like I had done some cardio work. The only thing I was missing was the fresh air and view. I still did my coastline visits, though I did not spend as much time doing them, and I was mainly in the car as the passenger. This was one of my sacrifices in becoming the new me. I had to see all the positives in the changes I had to make. It's so easy to destroy what you can achieve with a negative attitude and outlook.

People telling me throughout my recovery that I can achieve the task in action when I know I really can't is really upsetting. I can think about what I want to do but putting that thought into practice was a whole different story.

Throughout my recovery, I never pondered the question, "Why me?" I'd be lying if I said I never questioned the situation. However, it was more of a question like, "How long is recovery?" The million-dollar question was like asking how long a piece of string is - a question that never gets answered.

A common statement you hear when in the position of acquiring a brain injury is that no two brain injuries are the same. There are so many variations towards bleeds within or on the brain that it is almost impossible to advise when it comes to the healing timescale. We are all affected differently when it comes to the area of concern. We must not lose sight of our personal recovery time frames. Just because we don't reach our peak recovery in our suggested time frames does not mean we stop recovering.

It all came down to having a positive attitude towards the situation; some may say it is easier said than done, which at some points it was. Though I was in the frame of mind that I couldn't change what happened, it happened; it even appears to have been issued to me at birth. I always believed there was a light at the end of the ever-long tunnel; that was something I never stopped believing, and I was going to reach it. That was my goal; that was my path.

I don't like to big myself up, but I had to be bold to get through the effects of my brain haemorrhage. I had to stay motivated, enthusiastic and determined if I wanted results. My recovery wasn't a case of days or weeks; it was a case of years.

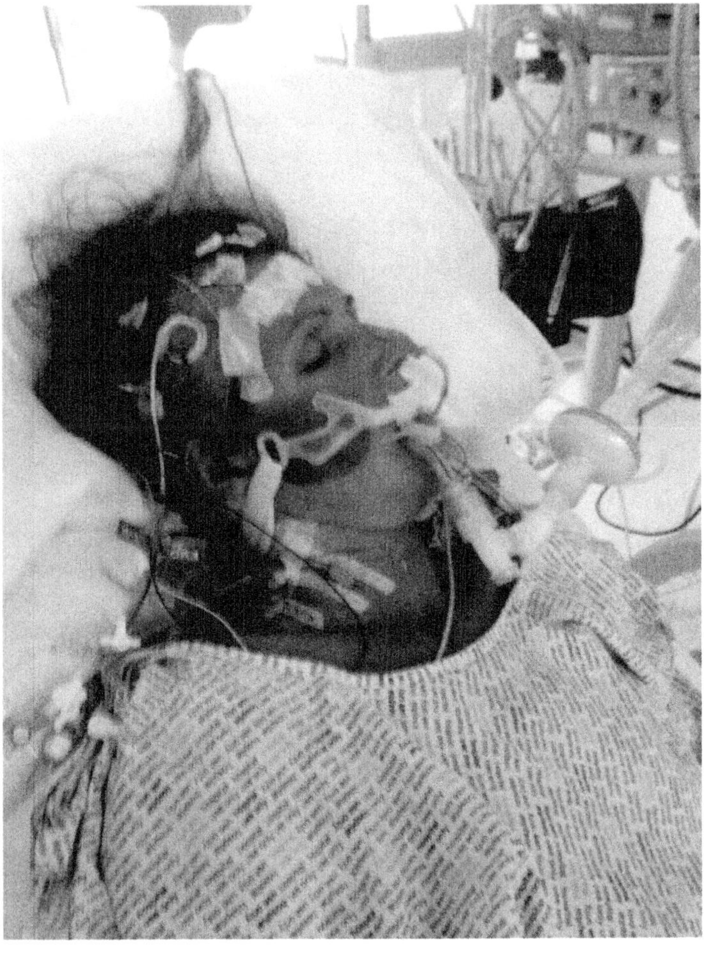

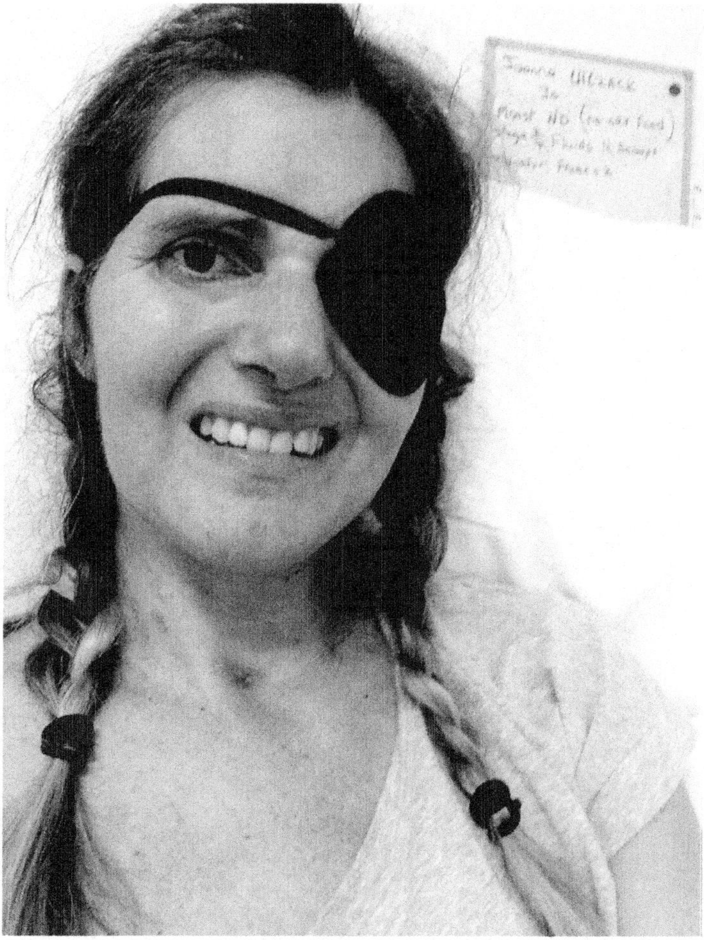

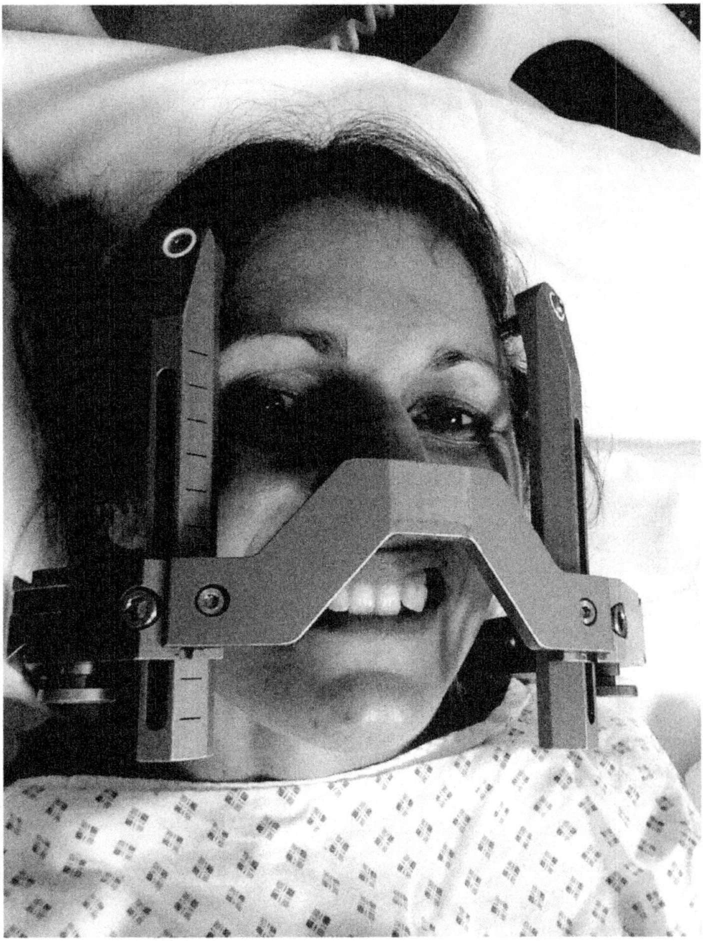

"The steps you take don't need to be big they just need to take you in the right direction."

Marvels Agents of S.H.I.E.L.D

Chapter Two | My AVM

So again, the question is, where do you start with a story like mine? I hear you say the beginning would be a good place, but it's hard to determine the beginning as I have lived with the condition my entire life. I processed information on situations and illnesses which would have evolved only due to processing an AVM. I will start with my first known bleed back in 2015. My life changed in October 2015. I woke in the early hours of the morning with chronic back-of-head pain and feeling like I had food poisoning; I had lost all taste as my taste buds had been affected. I somehow made my way to the bathroom, which was luckily next to my bedroom. I couldn't be sick even though I had the sensation to be, and my head was a led weight. I knew something was incorrect with my health. I was not feeling right; it wasn't just a sensation of being unwell. I asked my mum to stay with me for the remainder of the night as my feelings convinced me something serious was happening. After that, I was unaware of how much my life would change.

My Mum informed me after this incident that she'd tried to get a doctor out as I'd behaved very peculiarly, for which they refused. They informed my Mum I had a virus. She wasn't in agreement as they hadn't even seen me. They also informed my Mum that she should take me to see them if I was no better by the afternoon. My Mum had no idea how she would achieve this, but she did. She transported me wearing my PJs and placed some slippers on my feet. It was too much of a mission to try and dress me. After being seen, I was diagnosed with suspected viral Meningitis, and they told me to go straight to A&E, which was around a twenty-five minutes drive away. By this point, my Mum was panicking. How would I manage a car journey? I couldn't even sit upright. The doctor made an appointment for us, and we went off.

The appointment was a waste of time as we still had to sit and wait. After around three hours, a doctor saw me and couldn't conclude what was happening. He called a senior doctor in and, after doing their assessment, was concerned something more serious was going on and put me forward for a CT scan. From this, they discovered the bleeding within the brain, and a helicopter airlifted me to another hospital. From this happening, from waking in the night, I lost my memory until I woke in hospital; I would have only been thirty-four years old.

It felt like something out of a movie when I first woke. I lay on my side looking forward; everything was out of focus, and I slowly became in focus. They had drilled into my skull to place a tube which would then drain fluid from the brain, also known as a burr hole. I had no idea what was happening; I was delusional and semiconscious. I spent two weeks in hospital, and it took me around a year to gain some strength and stamina again.

I hear you say, what is an AVM? This is a question which I also asked myself when the doctor first told me my brain consisted of one. I later learned AVM stands for Arterior Venous Malformation, which in English is a tangling of blood vessels found in different locations around the body, and for me, it was within my brain, well deep within my cerebellum, to be precise. How lucky was I, a brain malformation which was quite rare. If only it were that amazing. I happened to have my AVM in an area of the brain which was inoperable, so I had to undergo Stereotactic radiotherapy, also known as gamma knife, to destroy it. I can assure you that Stereotactic radiotherapy sounds more exciting and inquisitive than it actually is. In brief, it primarily consists of a metal frame that medics screw onto the head, which they use as a ruler like a measuring tool. They place a patient onto a machine, which is very similar to an MRI machine, and you undergo your required length of time, where they beam gamma radiotherapy onto the area of concern. The outcome of this treatment is that the radiotherapy shrinks the area of concern to zero over a handful of years.

My second bleed happened on the first of June 2017, exactly five months after I had received treatment for my first bleed, which took over a year for an appointment. This bleed was ten times worse than my previous bleed.

It was a normal work morning and felt like any other typical day. I had not long joined the local doctor's practice in the administration department. I was working on reception on this particular morning and checking patients in. I was helping one patient, and I noticed that my vision had changed dramatically when I looked at my computer screen. I went to the back room and was a little concerned as it had just come on abruptly. My vision started shaking quite viciously, and it went slightly blurred. I saw plenty of floaters in my vision, and a hot fever began. One of my colleagues took me to an unoccupied room, where I lay down. I started feeling nauseous, though I wasn't actually sick. I got back up as the symptoms were not easing.

A sense of familiarity occurred as if I had experienced something similar before. I informed my colleagues of my thoughts; 'it's happening again; my AVM is bleeding.' I lost my memory from this point onwards, only to start becoming conscious again two months on. My family and friends filled me in on the blanks; my immediate description is based on their memories. I was extremely fortunate to work where I was, acquiring immediate care and first-hand attention. And even more so, to have an ambulance on site, which would not always be the case. I must thank my stars to the companies who never employed me when I was job searching. If it wasn't for their rejection of job opportunities, our local surgery would not have employed me, and I may not have even survived the bleed due to not receiving professional knowledge and urgent attention. That's how delicate my situation was.

I was ambulanced over to our local hospital, where they discovered a bleed was occurring. Then, the staff arranged for a helicopter to airlift me to the nearest hospital, which handled neurology concerns. I was extremely gutted to discover I had been in a helicopter twice now and had no recollection of this experience.

I spent two and half months in the hospital as opposed to my two-week stay with the first incident. The first month saw the medical ICU team place me into an induced coma for survival purposes as my body was fast shutting down. I was temperature-controlled and, at times, packed in ice. The staff eventually eased off the breathing equipment. If I could perform breathing without the equipment, I was moving in the right direction. Thankfully, I was moving in the right direction. After the ICU ward, I moved into a recovery ward where the medical team monitored me and later moved me to a hospital which was local to my home. I stayed stationed here until a rehabilitation hospital became available, which didn't take longer than a week to acquire. I spent just over a month in the rehab hospital before I was released home.

Smiling was my only expression for the world. It was quite ironic, as in, who wishes to smile out loud when trauma has disrupted your life? I could not achieve any other expressions. My face was extremely tight and wrinkle-free free I might add. All I could think was that it was cheaper than Botox but not a nice way to have wrinkle-free skin. I can assure you all my wrinkles came back with time. Before my second bleed, I felt at my fittest. I was smiling massively regarding this. I had fought my entire life for a taste of energy. Upon waking in the hospital from my second bleed, my body was in shock, and the best way it could express this was through smiling. My brain was in denial of the trauma which had occurred and neither were prepared for the long journey which lay ahead.

My favourite line would be, *"It is what it is."* If anyone ever questioned my feelings about something, I would simply reply with this line. I knew my incident was not self-inflicted; I did not abuse my body or was involved in an accident to my body. It was an unfortunate natural occurrence, one which no one would have known existed in my body if this bleed had not happened.

When I was finally discharged, I wasn't walking freely, I hardly had the strength to stand. Not that I could stand alone; I had to be supported. It was even hard for me with a form of walking aid. I basically did not have the strength to perform the standing action. It took me a good few months to stand up straight. I had to teach the brain the simplest of tasks from absolute scratch. I had to go back further than a baby learning its first encounters in life. I saw the situation in that a baby has pathways already created within the brain, which just requires them to be filled with a learning pattern. I did not have the pathways as the bleed had destroyed them (it reminds me of a volcano erupting and the flowing lava destroying villages in its path; that's my AVM erupting and destroying nearby pathways with its flowing blood.) I now had to create new pathways and fill them with exciting patterns, which would be sufficient for the human body. This results in the brain having two jobs rather than just one. I had to draw and paint the picture rather than just paint. Life had not awarded me a colour-by-numbers book.

If it weren't for my parents caring for me and supporting me like they did, I would have been pretty stuck. I don't actually know what I would have done. I needed twenty-four-hour assistance, and due to my poor vision and lack of walking ability, I made daily living quite discomforting.

If not having an ounce of independence wasn't depressing enough, I don't know what was. I was unable to venture anywhere alone. I always had company; well, I was in a wheelchair in my early months. I wasn't fortunate enough to honour enough stability in my mobility for venturing as and when on my own accord. I couldn't get a lift somewhere to venture to my destination alone. When I could take steps, I had to be walked into the destination and assisted throughout. I contended with this for four years. It then became slightly easier as I needed less assistance. I still wasn't walking independently, though I was managing a good few steps, enabling me a snippet of independence.

From my personal experience, my thoughts and views on an AVM are that no one really understands one. I believed I would get better and never stopped this chain of thought. I was no medic, though the brain becoming damaged released a confident approach to my situation and circumstance. It released an understanding towards the body. With this understanding, I could not see why it couldn't heal itself. I did believe it would happen much sooner than it did. However, over time, I relaxed towards the slow approach and appreciated that it was improving. It takes time to accept. Only at my two-year mark did I start becoming more relaxed with the speed of my recovery. I always felt I would go to bed and wake up with some major improvement. Unfortunately for me, it never happened that way. I would go to bed and wake up feeling like the day before. I would acknowledge all improvements achieved and talk myself through them. Seeing how hard it was to walk outside, we obviously take our walking ability for granted. I struggled enormously; any little incline or decline within the pavement or stone that got under my footwear was enough to send me walking into a drunken dance. It was by no means easy for me to attempt a walk. It occurred to me during April 2020 how much I had slipped into accepting the idea of assisted walking. I no longer thought of how I used to pop out from home to carry out my daily errands. These choices were not currently available to me, and they hadn't been to this point of nearly three years post-bleed, and it was still ongoing.

I had not forgotten but had not considered doing errands due to my limited capabilities. My daily venture outside incurred every time, a form of walking difficulty. No matter how difficult it was, I held tight to the idea of improving everything. I never believed my independence was unachievable. It was slower than I had imagined, but it was never unachievable. Honestly, at this point, I had no real idea what was achievable and what was not. I just strongly believed I could do it. Our brains are so magnificent that we can achieve whatever we wish, considering we put time and effort into it.

Acquiring a brain injury somehow offered me new superpowers. All situations had obvious answers. We could all say that there are obvious paths to follow in certain situations, but how often do we actually pursue the path? However, I calculated my new confidence with all the effects on others involved without thinking about the situation. I started to have a voice, and I was no longer hiding in the shadows, creeping around silently (not in a weird way). I wanted centre stage so I could say my piece. I'm sure some individuals found me a nightmare; they much preferred me to stay silent in the shadows. I had already lived there and can't say it was the right place for me. You tend to bottle up emotions and opinions when you have a quiet personality. You keep them close and don't share. You don't want others to question you on your opinions. You just want to live an easy, straightforward life.

After my brain bleed, I became quite the opposite. I wanted others to question my opinions; I was no longer concerned about what others may think of my ways of thinking. After all, it was only my opinion and how I looked at the situation. I was seeing the obvious right and wrongs. Before my bleed, I may have justified answers and used my compassionate emotions towards situations; now, I was blunt in my ways. I wasn't now going to ask a question and wait how many days for an answer. I wanted the answer now. As the saying goes, time waits for no man, and it's true. I had spent thirty-six years living one way; I was now seeing its faults, and after being offered a second chance, I would live my life more confidently.

Of course, over time, this new confident demeanour lessened. The more time went on, the more my compassionate emotions returned. In the early months, you can clearly see all the circumstances that have possibly helped you achieve the bleed. You want to see justification for these past situations. Even though I knew it was a birth development which could have bled at any time or not at all. It was a lottery. I had to live as normal a life as possible. I had to participate in daily activities such as visiting the supermarket to keep up with society. It was hard, that's for sure. I couldn't walk independently, so I relied on having a trolley to push, which my balance required. However, I also couldn't walk far, and I could not see clearly. I had to guess my path most of the time. I couldn't manage the whole store, but if I could walk an aisle with a trolley, it was an achievement.

There seems to be very little knowledge of the type of haemorrhage which I happened to endure. Seeking out help and advice was a true struggle. There was minimal advice and help services on offer. Not even for the people caring for you. An AVM is known to be a rare type of cause of haemorrhage, resulting in very little guidance. While going through the initial recovery process, which took a good few years, you realise that you can't give much aftercare on recovery, as the body heals as and when the brain wants it to. For example, I would go to the gym assisted a couple of times a week to keep my muscle strength. It wouldn't matter if I chose to go twice a week or five times a week; my outcome would be exactly the same. It took a very long time before the brain became interested in what I was doing. I started the gym as a shaking mess. I had to be assisted around the gym and helped with the machinery for getting on and off and weight selection. After two years of continually going a couple of times a week, I could roam around a little on my own accord. I was still awkward in my ways and needed assistance, but I was a little more independent. I decided to continue with my attendance for the foreseeable future, with the goal of continual improvement. The improvement kind of shone a light on the idea that the gym was super beneficial; my muscles had strengthened even though they felt unworked most of the time.

The most unwelcome piece of positive information, which I would quite often receive, and I'm not ungrateful, I just wish I was as good as it looked: 'You're doing really well, look how good you're doing'. As much as I appreciated the words spoken, I was in immense pain within. My entire body would hurt, and my brain would be challenged psychologically. The brain was receiving so much information regarding my attempt at walking that making it look good came at a cost. On the outside looking at me no one could see this, well maybe on some occasions. No one could see that I swayed intensely within, that my knees couldn't handle my weight and created pain, and that my calf muscles felt knotted and twisted and wanted to explode. Any movement of my eyes made me want to head butt in that direction. I couldn't see the path that I was walking with ease, so if it dipped or stepped up, I had no idea if a pavement was coming up etc. I was manually walking my left leg as it's not automatic to walk, and I had to determine all information about the terrain as any passing noises were enough to throw all abilities out the window and so on... I think I have painted the picture.

Anyone can have an AVM, and the chances of it bleeding are unpredictable. The chances of even discovering an AVM are extremely rare, as they are hard to detect, and you can go your entire life processing one and be none the wiser to its existence within the body.

In the immediate time after my bleeds, I was in denial of what had happened to me. I was living and my mindset was as if the bleeds hadn't happened, instead of accepting my new limitations. However, I was unaware of new limitations as I was still so unsteady in my ways and had nothing to work with in helping me adapt to new ways of living. My new way of living didn't really happen until five years passed. I would say confidence is what helped me accept the new me.

I was extremely disheartened by the lack of support and guidance after both my bleeds and being discharged from the hospital. I felt as though I was passed over to someone else continually. It was as if no one showed any interest in my recovery, yet my daily living was a struggle. I took it upon myself to seek answers, as I wouldn't accept the lack of communication I received. I was persistent in my rehabilitation and I was now persistent in my questions with seeking guidance towards recovery. No one understood my condition and symptoms and I was ready to explain myself. I discovered that you must be categorised as a stroke survivor to receive any aftercare. If you present yourself as having a brain haemorrhage, it's not recognised. It's quite ironic, considering how life-threatening a brain haemorrhage is, if you have survived a bleed within the brain, you would expect a form of aftercare. Sadly, this isn't the case, though to present yourself as a stroke survivor, you receive ample aftercare. In my understanding as much as they are similar, they are different. For me, my brain haemorrhage did offer me stroke symptoms as in my left side was damaged. You will discover this later on.

Upon coming home, I had to be wheelchaired everywhere. I would say I had a good six to twelve months of being wheelchaired about; after this time, I decided to ditch the chair. I wanted to get better and felt that relying on the wheelchair would only hinder this. It only came out if it was a real necessity. It just wasn't me to be wheeled about as I wanted my independence, and I was prepared to get to the next stage at whatever cost. I had no body strength and struggled to sit up from lying down, so I worked on my core by doing daily core-building exercises. However, this was not an overnight fix, as it took months to achieve some posture. My Dad gave me the greatest mobility help - he never gave up on me improving. It was easy to give up, but to keep going took strength and a bold personality. In time, I was not independent, but I could walk with assistance from another person. I had discovered a walking aid was a hindrance. My brain couldn't multitask, so thinking about something other than walking was hard work. Walking itself took all my strength and energy. Also, the brain was so powerful that if it wanted to see me fail or topple over I would. No walking aid was going to help prevent that from happening.

The medical team will advise you with suggested time frames for recovery but remember that they are only suggestions and not set in stone. My consultant informed me that it would reveal if recovery would or could happen within the first six months. The most apparent recovery happens within this window, and they can see if you can repair yourself to whatever extent that may be. It may take another two years, which is when the healing process can occur. You do have to remember that when you hit two years, you don't just stop repairing. Recovery and repair are ongoing. The following years show the continued recovery, though it was unfortunate that this was slow for me. Medics saw me repair, but because I was in such a bad condition, they viewed the first six-month window as more of a survival window.

Even though my bleed damaged my cerebellum to a degree that it was unrepairable, I never lost my memories. I always knew how to carry out tasks and how walking was supposed to happen. I don't know if this went against my recovery as I was always comparing myself or whether it was a positive towards my recovery as it was guiding me. Sometimes, it's best to forget what you know and start from scratch; other times, knowing how to carry out a task is very informative.

"Can I be bothered with the day ahead?" I quite often asked myself this question each morning. It was more "Have I got the strength for the day ahead?" I knew that from the moment I stepped out of bed, my efforts would be pushed to their limits. The most common sentence I would repeatedly say was, "When am I going to get better?" The million-dollar question (why do we say dollar when we are pounds? Baffles me.)

"The brain is seen as a power tool which controls all movements. I have no thought process of my own to override its actions. The brain can't be overridden. It will make unexpected actions to movements."

Jo Ulczak

Chapter Three

Sensations and Post-Bleed Symptoms

Easy is an understatement.

Throughout my recovery, I experienced many different forms of sensations, emotions, feelings, understandings, patience, compassionate states, relationships, and so forth. It was like the brain had tapped into untouched areas/territories, which showed different understandings of situations.

My four predominant symptoms, which were hugely disruptive to my daily living, were my vision, balance, my inner body sway and my walking. From day one, I believed that if my vision were correct, it would have a knock-on effect on my other symptoms. This proved not to be the case. I started to label the situation as 'the sponge effect'. I absorbed all symptoms at the same pace. In my case, it proved there was no release of any one symptom to edge on the recovery of another. I had to wait for them all to heal at the same speed.

My most commonly known symptoms included internal swaying (inner body sway as I called it), shaking, a warm back of the head, tight forehead, can't lay on a side as it pulled backwards, loss of taste, poor swallowing, moving brain sensations, damaged sinuses, nasal congestion, poor walking ability, weak lower legs even though exercised, sore heels, poor balance and damaged vision. Some symptoms started to ease after two years, though they never improved one hundred per cent, and many stayed with me for many years.

I suffered from swollen feet for the first three months of being home. They would go dark red with a hint of purple and were very sensitive. The surfaces on which I walked had a huge impact on them, and this lasted for years after the bleed to this day. I couldn't stand in the shower or on any wet flooring as I perceived them as extremely slippery. I would have a stool, shower mat and a grab rail for safety in the shower. My feet struggled with grip. I wore neoprene beach shoes for stepping on wet surfaces, and their rubber sole offered a safety net for me as they would stop the slipping feeling I felt. When walking outside, I felt minor stones trapped under my footwear. I could not wear footwear that didn't support my foot - my feet had to be strapped in. Closed shoes were the comfiest and safest. I could not multitask, so thinking about what my footwear was doing, alongside the actual walking, was a massive no-no.

One time, I had badly rubbed between my toes from my flip flops, which had a back strap to support it on the foot, so I replaced these with a pair of flip flops which had one strap across the toes. You usually see people at swimming pools wearing one-strap flip flops; I think they are known as sliders. I didn't realise this when I purchased them, but my left foot could not hold the flip flop and continually kicked it off. I, of course, would have to take light to this despite how much it actually upset me, and I would change my footwear for some closed-in shoes. My flip flop days were gone. I found myself living in trainers post-bleed as they were the comfiest footwear. I couldn't wear running trainers as they offered too much rock in the front of my foot, which would have me catapulting forward due to my balance. The trainers only offered a slight rock motion. The flat trainer felt like I was wearing snowshoes. It was a minefield trying to find the perfect fit.

One of the biggest problems I would incur is that individuals around me would not understand that I sometimes don't control my movements. For example, I'd practice walking independently on our quiet street, and a vehicle would come by. I'm informed to step onto the pavement due to walking on the empty road; I would do so and discover that the pavement was on a slant, which would send my brain into a frenzy, spinning me around and off balance. The brain can't multitask as it has received multiple instructions. I would shout for a form of help; otherwise, I would be seen to fall. My assistant did not understand that I could not override the brain's actions when it panicked. As much as I would like to be able to override its actions, I simply can't. It's super awkward when these symptoms reveal themselves, as I have no control over their actions.

I would often say with an undiagnosed symptom, "I will add it to my list of never-ending symptoms...." it was what I felt I had to do. No one seemed to have much advice on what I would say to them regarding my symptoms.

My day would be over by ten a.m. as I had no energy left for the remaining hours from my efforts in getting up. This energy zap would not impact my sleep pattern, though - I only wish it did. I never slept during the day. The only time my brain switched off was when it knew I had gone to bed. It was so frustrating. I would be so tired during the day that I just couldn't sleep. My body never relaxed. I could go for a laydown, but my body would shake internally. So, to look at me, I was laying still, though internally, I was springing about. My brain would be making its own sensation as this changed quite often. I would want to cry, but I couldn't express this emotion. I just wanted to be still and calm - something which only proved to be a wish. I contended this every day for forty months post bleed. After this time, I was still not internally still, though I had calmed enough to feel satisfied with the sensation.

I am going to categorise my symptoms to help you understand my most challenging contenders more clearly; the following will include examples and diary logs. Two of my main symptoms were walking and balance; I have given these two categories their own chapters.

No one knew how well I would recover. Everyone admittedly said they really didn't know how recovery would appear, and some were amazed I had survived the initial attack. As much as this was disheartening to hear in the moment, it never halted my strive towards recovery.

I had video footage taken of myself to remind me how far I had come on my low-mood days and how much I had improved. Even though I may be finding it really hard, I was slightly closer to the end goal. I highly recommend videoing yourself. It lifts your mood.

1 - Hearing - ear defenders at the ready

In my immediate months post-bleed, my hearing was on sensory overload. My circumstances heightened everything in sound. No one had any privacy if near me. I could hear all conversations within the home, even if at opposite ends of the house. I had tapped into an area of hearing we seem to bypass as humans. When we witness other species on high alert for their hearing, for example, a cat when it's hunting, their ears are like radar's continually moving and picking up every possible sound. I was now the cat without the moving ears; I might add, collecting all noises.

I struggled to watch TV as it had to be on a whisper, along with my damaged vision. It was not much fun for my company as they now couldn't hear it. I had one friend who would call over quite often to watch some TV and keep me company for a bit, as I saw very few people during my immediate recovery time. I take my hat off to them for being kind and sitting with me even if they couldn't hear the TV. That takes a lot of patience. Watching a series when you can't even grasp what's going on as you can't hear it is pretty frustrating if nothing else. Although I was always kindly informed they could hear the TV fine.

Most days, my parents would try to spend some time in the outside air; no one wants to be continually trapped indoors. I was fortunate that I had parents who enjoyed being outside. This proved very beneficial, though somewhat hard work, as I could hear cars that would be three streets away sounding like they were on the street on which we would be walking. Also, passers-by would be distracting as their heightened footsteps were noisy and extremely off-putting to what I would have been trying to achieve. Of course, the passer-by would not understand that they were off-putting to my dealings.

I also occasionally received high-pitched noises in my left ear, which was very frustrating. The noise never lasted all day, but it was still very uncomfortable. I thought maybe noise cancelling earplugs would help. After researching and reading forums regarding heightened hearing, I purchased myself some of these earplugs. I thought they dampened the noise with your surroundings; only I found them to cancel out all noise. Fantastic if you want a good night's sleep. I found them slightly dangerous in my situation as I didn't have the reactions and balance to see me dodge danger. I decided against them, but for sleeping, they were a blessing.

2 - Taste, speech and nasal passage

From the beginning, both my taste and my speech were damaged. In my early days, the taste of dairy products affected me. I had to replace butter and milk with alternatives like soya and oat. The dairy taste used to burn my mouth. Strangely, I could eat super-hot chillies; to me, it was like eating a piece of lettuce. The doctor advised me that eating strong-tasting spices and herbs could do a very good job of stimulating my taste buds back into action. For me this was not the case. On the plus side, I was very good at eating extremely strong-tasting spiced food. If only there was a competition for this. I lost most of my taste buds; I would describe it as I had just had a hot tea bag in my mouth, and this sensation I felt after eating any form of food. It wasn't the pleasantest, though I got on with it. I had to eat after all. One taste bud I remember losing was my sweet one. I no longer required sugar in my tea or coffee; sweet cereals like Cheerios, biscuits and cakes were a no-go; basically, the body no longer enjoyed anything with a high sugar consistency. To some, this would not be an issue; to others, it would be unbearable. I took it as a blessing, as I'm sure I would have easily put on weight, as there was not a lot I could do to burn the calories.

I suffered quite badly with my teeth clasping together. This lasted a good few years post-bleed. It slowly reduced after this time, seeing them only occasionally smacking together. It would mainly happen if tired or cold. I would lie in bed at night, and my teeth would chatter away. I wasn't even cold.

I had to train myself not to have my teeth touch when going to sleep as this encouraged the action to take place. It was uncomfortable at times as the action would happen from nowhere, and I was always in fear of incurring a form of tooth damage. Even when I had reached four years post-bleed, my front teeth would still cross paths and smack one another.

My speech was quite nasally in the beginning. I used to feel as though I had some damage within my nasal passages, as it felt as though I spoke through my nose. Over time, this eased away, and my speech improved. I still felt as though my nasal passage was hindered in some way, but we never got to the bottom of it. I started using nasal cold and flu sprays, which I found extremely helpful in clearing my nasal passages. This allowed my speech to stay normal and less nasally.

As with my teeth clasping when tired, this was the same for my speech. The more tired I became, the more my speech became slurry. It was a dead giveaway as to when I was tired due to my struggle with speaking. When I had passed five years, I was still struggling with my speech. I was in the sixth-year post-bleed, and I would get extremely cold to the point I would struggle to speak even if it was slightly cold or even just cool outside. I would wrap up extra warm even when you wouldn't expect it. I couldn't afford to get cold and allow my outside time to be over.

I also had quite a sensitive throat. I couldn't move my head when eating, as this would trigger a cough. I struggled to swallow on many occasions; even when I had surpassed six years, I would on occasion struggle to swallow. For example, on a routine dentist visit, holding your mouth open generates fluid that trickles down your throat. I would wish to swallow, but I couldn't. My reflexes in my throat didn't respond to commands.

3 - Sight - blinkers

In my early days post-bleed, my eye sockets became extremely drawn. My right eye socket had an inverted effect, while my left one had kind of risen. I had incurred the dark shadow effect, and they looked unwell. Over the years, it did slightly improve, and the shadows became less, although I had to resort to face paint to help hide the evidence of dark circles.

My sight was a major issue for me as it was extremely damaged. I wasn't blind, though I couldn't see correctly. Explaining what I could see proved extremely difficult when speaking to specialists. No one seemed to understand. It wasn't until I reached three years post-bleed that I saw improvement in this area. That's three years where I struggled with my sight to the degree of almost being blind as the processing process of the vision to the brain was so slow; friends and family guided me on where to step. They talked me through what I was required to do, such as stepping off or onto a pavement, preparing for a slight incline or decline in my path, whether gravel or grass terrain was approaching, etc. I couldn't see the food on my plate and only deciphered it by out-of-focus colours. This took over a year to improve slightly, as it next moved onto room lighting being the issue. If the room was too dim, I may not be able to see my plate of food correctly. Lighting always played a major part in my activities. I was always slightly sensitive to lighting, even before my bleed. At three years post-bleed, I would say I could see my plate of food, even with dysfunctional lighting. Though I had to be in good form to achieve this, I would struggle if I was slightly tired.

In my early days of being home from the hospital, I remember waking in the morning and looking up at the ceiling and seeing two lights. I would will myself to heal so I would only see one light on the ceiling. Three and a half years later, I was still seeing the two lights on my bedroom ceiling upon waking; I even noted that at five years post-bleed, I was still seeing two lights. My vision had improved slightly, though not on my morning double vision.

For me, explaining my linked eye and brain sensation was extremely hard. I could see and determine the image, but at the same time, I didn't always see the whole picture with my left eye. For example, if there was a bird in my vision, I may not always see the bird. But if I stared long enough, I would see the bird. The left eye would feel super uncomfortable, and I would get an angled image that overlapped my right eye vision. If I ever patched it, I would see perfectly fine with my right eye, yet if I patched off my right eye, I could see perfectly fine with my left eye, though it did feel like the left eye worked harder. The sensation from the eye is something I can't explain, except it was super uncomfortable. Across the left side of the brain, it was also uncomfortable. The eye itself actually hurt and disagreed with most light.

I've contended with double vision, also known as diplopia, to this day post-bleed. In my first-year post-bleed, if I went out anywhere, I would wear a patch on my left eye, which was my damaged eye. It would help me see the picture clearer. The brain felt unsettled, therefore making the vision unsettled. It seemed the eyes didn't align, so the brain received two images. One image I received was straight, and the second image was distorted. I did get pointed at and called a pirate on occasions by younger children, which made me chuckle. On one occasion, a lady assumed I had lost my eye. As heartbreaking as it was, I knew wearing a patch to get through my day seeing correctly was my best option. After about three years, my distorted picture started to become transparent, but it is still there.

If someone was to say, 'Look at that bird on the rock,' for example, I would have to search for the bird and by the time the brain had found it and processed it, it would have gone resulting in not actually seeing the bird for any length of time but instead using endless amounts of energy to carry out a simple task. My improvement with my sight didn't happen in any imaginable way. It became slightly sharper and steadier over time, meaning years. My distorted image started to become transparent, and the two images started to merge.

I tried as much as possible not to wear the patch as I felt it would only strengthen the left eye. Doing this was hard as my eyes became tired and refused to work. The eye muscles would hurt, and I would get headaches in my temples. I experienced a lot of strained eyes as they would go quite red and bloodshot, too. Being in the sunshine would have this effect even while wearing sunglasses. It was very off-putting for me to go outside. Looking at a TV or computer was extremely hard, and my phone usage became minimal. Nothing was worth the aftermath of the pain it created.

My sight wasn't really manageable for the remainder of 2017. I would describe it as a 'flicked ruler vision'. My eyes were the end of a flicked ruler, which would cause the ruler's end to flicker vigorously. A year and a half on, I was still struggling; my vision was blurred and out of focus. I could look forward but not sideways or turn my head to look behind me, and my vision was often very spirally like a Mozart painting. I had to stare quite badly to absorb the image, it was as if the processing of the vision signal was the issue. I could see but it was very impaired and slow at processing the information. I was unable to judge depth and distance. By the end of 2018, it had slightly improved, though I still had much more improvement.

I couldn't read for the first few years; my parents had to do everything for me. I could manage a sentence or two in my second year, though completing this simple task would take all my energy. I attempted to read a book with a larger font after three years, but my double vision was quite a hindrance.

I never knew which line started the next sentence, and the words were out of focus. I would read with a ruler to know what sentence I should read. My parents would read aloud to me if any important reading were required.

If I had to concentrate, I would lose my vision, and much of what I would do would be through guesswork and memory. I couldn't look behind me in my early stages as there was no vision for this action. I started to believe it was because whatever was behind me wasn't important. Therefore, I didn't waste my energy trying to piece together an image. It would have been kind of frustrating if the light switch was behind me, but that's another story.

Glasses were of no help because if my eyes didn't want to focus, they wouldn't. Not even wearing glasses would help, and when I patched an eye off, it wouldn't encourage the eye to focus. This led me to believe it was the brain causing these concerns, not the eyes themselves. Also, according to my optician, my eyes were healthy.

I have not cried to this day, and I'm past six years - unless the cold air or wind made my eyes water. I cried a lot inside, but I could not express this emotion externally. Upon coming home from the hospital, I used prescribed eye drops to help keep them lubricated, as they would feel very uncomfortable by the end of the day.

Close-up images were extremely detailed during my first year. I could even see every detail on a bumble bee that would fly past me extremely slowly, and I would question if I had seen everything too quickly in its movement. It was like all wildlife was on a go-slow approach as I watched garden birds move about, and there was minimal movement in the garden. I witnessed images in my peripheral vision that weren't actually there. I could be sitting on the sofa attempting to watch TV, and I would see the cat enter the room, only the cat was outside. The mind likes to imagine possibilities.

Some days, my brain realised that the left eye's vision was completely separate from the right. It took around twenty months before the left eye started to open up. It still needed to be corrected, but its appearance improved. Even after five years, the left eye and brow slanted slightly.

Upon waking some mornings, I would have a stinging sensation in my left eye for no apparent reason. After it had been closed for several hours during sleep, I used some eye drops to help moisten it, though this only encouraged intense stinging. It was almost like I'd scratched the eye lens and was aggravating it. To this day, I don't understand why my eye was like this on waking.

During my first-year post-bleed, I taped my left eyebrow up to my forehead when going to bed. I wanted to open my eye more; it always looked like I was winking. I believed this would help train the eyebrow muscles to lift slightly. I don't believe it did anything. Medical staff gave me some eye exercises, which I did for a bit. However, I wasn't convinced they were aiding the situation, but at the same time, I thought they weren't doing any harm. I started the eye exercises again in February 2019 after taking a break from them. The eyes had corrected a bit, but I was still experiencing Nystigmas when looking sideways and double vision from any angle. I hoped the exercises would help both conditions, though I can't confidently say they helped.

During the same year, I noted to myself, whilst on a walk with my parents, how I would miss the centre section of the image I saw. Imagine three squares of paper held up in front of you. The square to the left is what the left eye sees, the square to the right is what the right eye sees, and the centre square joins them together. I was missing the centre square from my vision. We walked along a local coast path, and my Dad was upfront, seeking out the best path to follow for me and my Mum, who assisted me in my wheelchair as I couldn't manage longer walks on foot. I realised I couldn't see my Dad and the footpath he took; I could only see the long grass on either side of the path. Not seeing the full picture made my daily dealings extremely hard. I am pleased to state that this was only temporary and short-lived for a couple of years.

Diary Entry - 28/7/2019

Sight improvement - I could see my reflection enough after two years to apply some mascara. My first attempt at any form of make-up was mascara in July 2019. After this, I started to wear some mascara and eyeliner on occasion. I couldn't see correctly to try and apply any make-up until now. I still couldn't see one hundred per cent correctly, but I had enough correct sight to apply some basics; I may have involved a bit of guesswork, and some days, I may have looked connected to a panda family. However, it still made me feel part of humanity again. No matter how small my achievement was, it was more than enough.

Diary Entry - 2019

October 2019 - my eyes sometimes feel like they are sweating. It took two years before they would water but wouldn't cry. I would have to do the wide eye look to myself throughout the day, as I felt it helped to open the left eye up.

Vision signal:

The signal was super slow, it was no fibre optics that's for sure. I could be placed in front of a blue wall and asked what colour the wall was; the signal from the eyes to the brain and then brain to mouth was that slow. The conversation could now be two episodes on. I would endure headaches around the eyes, which felt like I had overworked the muscles. My eyes would feel uncomfortable and sore.

A year later, in 2020, I noticed more bounce within my eyes. One day, I was relaxing on my bed, looking out my window, when I noticed my drawn curtains. I shut one eye off, and this is when I realised I must drag the image when my eyes bounce sideways, as this was exactly what was happening. I would look at something, then look away and look back, dragging the image with my vision as the brain hadn't processed the image quickly, resulting in every time I looked away and then back, it added another picture to overlap the original picture. Another example of the drag effect could be looking out to sea and ending up with four horizons rather than one. It's hard with vision when the processing process is so slow. Some days, I would look at my feet, look away and look down again, and I would see two sets of feet as my mind hadn't moved on from the image of my feet before I looked away. Then I would not know which was the correct image. It was a tiring process.

Crossing the road, which involved looking left and right first, was almost impossible. I had to rely on sound. The vision signal was slow along with the seen image. I would drag the image by turning my head to create a blurred picture. I had no idea if there was a moving car in the image.

Try living for years without correct vision. That was me. When I was asked one day about my vision in December of that year, I noticed I could see 3D at times. It wasn't a permanent improvement as it only offered this function when it felt like it. When I looked at the pavement, I saw that the pavement was raised - something I couldn't see before.

I received no support or guidance for my vision situation, and it became clear that no one knew how to help. I used a lot of muscle power from around the eyes, which resulted in extreme fatigue in the front of my brain, even though this area was not affected. I would see an ophthalmologist who advised me my eyes were not in a condition where they could be helped. How was I expected to proceed when no one could offer any support?

Over the summer months, we would visit the beach from time to time, and while lying on the beach in the warm summer sun, I wouldn't be able to focus on the people sitting next to me. It was soul-destroying not being able to see what was happening around me. If I heard a noise, I wouldn't be able to react to it; if someone called, I was unable to see who it was; if the neighbouring beach sitters required assistance, I was unable to assist. I couldn't even get up onto my feet due to my mobility and meet family or friends on the shoreline, where they may be cooling down from the warm sun. I'd be stranded in the location for which I had been left.

The summer sun contributed to many headaches; they would usually be above the right eye, which was my strongest eye out of the two, and the entire front of my brain would hurt. The striking pain in my left eye through any sunlight was unbearable. It would sting and water and the whole eye would scream with a sharp pain that travelled to the back of my skull. No one knew of this pain unless I was to collapse to the floor, which never happened. I'd just smile, make a joke and carry on.

I often struggled with my eyes, continuously feeling as though they had grit in them. I would go to sleep with this sensation and then wake up with it. I had lubricant eye drops for them, which I used every night. On occasion, when they were sore during the day, the drops offered a moment of ease, and then I was back at the start. I struggled to find an answer.

The low winter sunlight was a massive setback for me. We all want to see the sun at any time of the year, but I was quite happy that it would disappear. Due to its winter's height in the sky, I was very blinded by it, making outside activities a major issue. I wore sunglasses, though this proved not to make the situation any easier. There was no solution; I had to sit it out and hope it would slowly improve. My left eye couldn't cope with the sunlight and would often freak the brain, allowing it to bear me to the left while walking or sending it into a spinning sensation.

Who would ever imagine vision would or could be painful? It's something we don't really express unless it's to do with lighting often involving the sun. It was over three years, and my left eye had still not corrected. It had improved but not corrected itself. Just vision alone would consume a huge amount of brain energy. It's hard to envision how getting up from bed early and walking across the house so extensively could wear the eyes out.

Diary Entry - 24/2/21

When I look down, I only see my feet opposed to four feet. It's not perfect and sharp, though the thought of now only seeing two feet is an improvement. When I place a pen in front of my eyes, I can now move it back and forth and see only one pen instead of two, with one version being distorted. Looking out my bedroom window, I see the garden set up much clearer. These are my acknowledgments that my vision is improving.

Diary Entries - April 2021

My vision becomes extremely tired extremely quickly. I lose the image ahead through tired eyes. If I look down, I'm okay, but then when I move to look forward, I lose the picture. If I stay looking forward, the picture emerges, though it takes some time to come into play. This is happening nearly four years post-bleed.

Sitting up front in the car was extremely hard for me during the first few years. Too much visual information was being processed by the brain, and it struggled to cope. I'd lose my vision because of this. I was a permanent backseat passenger. Occasionally, I liked to sit up front in the car as I wanted to see how my vision improved. I'd see the road ahead and hedgerow and I would also see it double at a slight angle. I always believed the doubled picture, which was slightly angled, would fade away. I was at year four and I still had the two images. However, I noticed that I didn't have a double vision for the hedgerow; it was for the road centre markings only. This wasn't how I imagined improvement would appear, though it was an improvement that made me happy.

On some occasions, I can only describe my vision as a misty day. You know those days when it's a nice day, and then the mist turns up? Everything is a haze, and as the mist thickens, objects that I can just about see fade out or simply get swallowed up by the mist. Looking at me, you would be unaware of how I was deciphering everything.

My vision was continually disheartening and a struggle as I had double vision, super light sensitivity and nystagmus at four-plus years. The positive I pieced together from this hardship was how my double vision was now aligned. For example, my double vision possessed one straight image and one distorted image placed to the side of the straight image. Now I saw the straight image with the double placed next to or above the straight image in alignment. There was no longer a distorted image. Seeing an improvement enabled me to believe improvement was taking place. Over the coming years, and yes, it would be years, as everything associated with brain repair occurs very slowly, I would have a much more stable vision outlook. I firmly held this belief.

Diary Entry - November 2021

I was unable to walk in dusk lighting. Now I'm managing it.

I was very good at closing my left eye - it was like I had a permanent wink. I was very good at this as I was unaware I was carrying out this action. I think the left eye closed itself from constantly seeing two images to make my vision that much easier. It was only ever my company in action which would point out this attractive look I shared. I continually achieved this for a good four years. Then, I noticed that I had received fewer comments regarding closed eyes. My vision had improved, resulting in me not having to close my eyes as much. I would only know of this improvement because I was no longer shutting my eyes as much, and it was being pointed out to me. Improvement was so subtle it would go unnoticed. When you receive information on improvement, you must explain to the brain that you are healing, and it happens very slowly. You must celebrate mentally and reward yourself with ample 'well done'; otherwise, it will go unnoticed or forgotten, and you won't realise how far you have come.

I'd struggle with reading my notes taken over the years and piecing my contents together as my eyes would struggle to focus. They would glaze over, and I would no longer be able to read my notes, yet I had only been reading for five minutes.

Around early 2023, I got some glasses with a frosted-out left lens to help with my double vision. For which it did. As time went on, I realised that I didn't always want to cover the left eye. Plus, onlookers continually informed me that my left lens had condensation. I revisited the opticians and got new glasses, but this time, I did not get the frosting. Instead, I purchased a patch which went on glasses. This allowed me to use it when I wanted, and I could also close the right eye off and force the left eye to work. I thought this would help to strengthen it, but I have no idea if it helped. For me, it wasn't a permanent solution to close off one eye, as some days it helped, and other days it was of no help, more of an annoyance.

4 - Spatial Awareness

I struggled with the awareness of my surroundings and my surrounding objects. I would be sitting out with some friends having a coffee, and I would not be able to judge the location of my cup on the table. I'd have to wave my hand over the table to find my cup and, at the same time, avoid knocking any cups and glasses over. When returning the cup to the table, I would need to find out where to safely place it, which often resulted in the cup falling over. I also did not recognise the distance I was sitting from my company.

With the walking link armed, I would never register the space between me and oncoming walkers or if they had a dog, for example. Onlookers didn't understand that I required space; they considered me rude. I quite often bashed into them.

5 - Brain sensations

I will start where the incident originates from - the brain. It has kept up displaying its existence in different forms.

I had many different sensations occur within the brain. The first example was within the first six months; this sensation was a rocking back-and-forth in the skull - almost like a rocking chair motion. I would pray for it to stop as it was most discomforting; I just wanted to cry constantly, though I couldn't express this emotion. It was so disheartening, and I struggled with the feeling of a moving brain for a few months. Once this sensation stopped, it only affected the area of concern, the left side of the cerebellum, and this area of the brain would move up and down in the back of the head. Well, that was the sensation it was radiating.

The sensation then mutated into what I could describe as an air bubble in a spirit level placed off balance - sideways or back and forth. This affected the entire brain, not just the area where the bleeding occurred. I contended with this for months.

Diary Entry

Throughout 2018, the back of my head continually felt very warm most of the time.

Two years later, I was still getting drawn to the left. The power of the brain is too mighty to override. No matter how much you know how to do something if the brain doesn't want to, it simply won't do it. It's frustrating when people around you continuously tell you that it's a simple task and you must tell the brain it can do it; if the brain chooses not to, it simply won't, no matter how easy the task is.

Another sensation was if you imagine an elastic band pulled tight and then flicked in the middle. The brain is in the middle, and the elastic band creates a juddering sensation. The juddering sensation has been present over the years, only received in a slightly different manner over time.

A sensation I would continually receive during the first three years was a pulsating/throbbing sensation within my cerebellum.

I would talk myself through the healing processes to how sensations would appear to me. It was, of course, not how it would be actually healing. It was just brain sensations in repair. When I first came home, I would go to sleep at night willing it to fix. I used to imagine it as a dot to dot, and it was joining up new pathways to heal. I then went through a phase of there being a black hole or void within the brain, which was unfixable. I then had the sensation that there was a dead circle shape within the brain, and it was requiring to be knitted back together. After this sensation, it was almost like there was a black hole within my brain, only involving strands which were hanging loosely off the non-damaged brain, getting knocked and vibrations sent through them.

I'd also have a heavy weight on the left side of my brain, which seemed to move about constantly. If I wanted to look down at the ground whilst walking and looking forward, there would be a good chance my head would pull me down, which I would have to try and not allow. Unfortunately for me, the brain did what it wanted.

Someone would take me down to the beach in the summer, and I would practice my assisted walking on the low-tide sand. I found this very beneficial as the beach offered plenty of space, and the sand was hard, making it easier to walk on than the continually moving dry sand. My area of brain injury felt like an area of void as I would feel nothing. It was like how I imagined a black hole with no feeling or emotion on offer. There was nothing there to act upon. I sometimes thought the area of concern was stitching itself back with the healing process. This was just my light-hearted take on it in my early stages, which I would say to myself as that is genuinely how it felt. The other healing take I would express is that the cerebellum is a sponge that absorbs all the injured areas.

Before this sensation, the cerebellum was very prominent in being unrelated to the rest of the brain; it felt dead.

The heat from a summer's day would really affect the brain; the brain did not welcome the warm sun. I had to live under umbrellas and wear hats to keep the sun off me.

I'd go to the swimming pool occasionally as I found this very positive regarding my recovery. One thing I always enjoyed before my bleed was swimming underwater, only now I couldn't perform this action as my head felt as though it was filled with helium; my head was a helium balloon being pushed underwater and wanting to resurface.

I would get brain judders from a sensation that felt like my cerebellum was a ball in water being pushed under and wanting to resurface, a bit like the brain sensation of going under water, only this sensation only involved the cerebellum, not the entire brain, and I wasn't in water.

During my second year, 2019, my cerebellum felt like one of those desktop metal ball games. The one that consists of three metal balls. You pull out the furthest left or right ball and swing it, and it knocks out the centre ball, which then knocks out the furthest left or right ball. That was my brain being jolted left and right within the back of the skull.

My continual problem was the gravitational pull at the back of the brain, which had been there since day one. I was not subjected to any pain, just a backwards-pulling sensation. An ongoing sensation to this day is how I get pulled backwards by the brain quite a bit. I could only describe this sensation as Spiderman shot his web at the back of your head and pulled you backwards, or your hair is pulled tight, and you are being pulled backwards by your hair. This sensation is appearing less and less, and it's been with me from the beginning.

I would often balance with one foot placed on a step; it's a simple action for someone with balance, and even after two and a half years, I was still getting pulled away and off the step by the brain. I was not unfit or too weak to carry out the task, it was just a case of the brain not wanting to know. It was down to this that my recovery with balance was hindered. My brain had taken a massive trauma and required a lot of patience and time to re-root itself.

Diary Entries - October 2019

I logged how it felt I was dealing with magnets in reference to the brain. I would receive the sensation of a heavy weight moving left and right within the skull. It felt like a magnet on the outside of the skull was pulling the head toward the magnet. This would make me fall off balance when trying to type rope balance, for example, placing one foot in front of the other. I had to continually try and override this sensation to enable me to balance. I had to imagine it not happening. It never really had the effect that I would like.

Late in the evening, around 10 pm, my brain would start playing up and bouncing about in the damaged area. I was no longer able to stay up late. It was all well and good going to bed early, but I didn't dream as I switched myself off for the night.

If the brain used both sides of its hemisphere, it would cause it to judder much more. For instance, if I used an arm rotation piece of gym equipment that required both arms, it would set my brain off. If I were to concentrate on using the opposite arm to the leg while walking, it would set the juddering off. It would only occur within the damaged area, though it was sometimes quite intense. It never really stopped while resting; it was just sometimes more prominent. It was almost like a droplet of water on a strand of cotton, setting the calmness of the strand off.

Over the years, post-bleed, I experienced completely fictional encounters. I would hear noises that never even happened. I would experience nighttime scenarios that saw me carry out actions, and sometimes, I never acted on these; it was all a thought process. I was hallucinating. On several occasions, I would get up at night to investigate a noise, be it a door lightly banging, the rain, the cat meowing, the doorbell, a conversation my parents would be having, the neighbours making noises in their garden, etc. On investigating, I'd experience the silence of the night. There was never anything suspicious going on. Occasionally, I would wake my parents to investigate the noise, which would miraculously disappear and reappear when they returned to bed. After three years of these experiences, I noticed that I woke in the early night hours. I acknowledged how it was very unlikely that whatever I was hearing was likely to happen. I believed it was all fictional within the brain. I hoped I could train my brain to switch off from these fantasy events. And then it all faded away.

When I reached a little over the four-year mark, I realised how much the brain had settled with my attempt at walking, and the head sensation had eased away. I was no longer getting thumped to the side in the back of the skull, be it left or right. It had reminded me of someone playing pinball in the back of my skull.

Diary Entry - 12/2/21

Today, I went on an extremely windy stroll with my parents, linked armed with my Dad, from Little Fistral Beach to North Fistral Beach and back. It was only a short walk which involved stopping and sitting down where possible, but the surf was good, and the sun was out. My parents questioned me on how my head felt with all the elements. Usually, going on past situations, it was perfect conditions to cause brain juddering. Still, today was the first time I had noted no juddering taking place. I would not have even noticed this if my parents hadn't questioned me about the symptoms. Once upon a time, I wouldn't have been able to go outside with even the slightest breezes. To be able to walk assisted on a windy day was a massive improvement but one which you could easily not acknowledge. Being a human spring doesn't make venturing out in the wind very inviting.

Diary Entry - May 2021

My head calmed slightly, and everything was still unsettled but more settled simultaneously. Improvement was super hard to see; it was only through searching and seeking it out that I noticed my improved abilities. I still practised placing my socks and shoes on while standing, a super hard action when you lack balance upon standing on one leg. I was still poor at managing this, but at the same time, I had improved with the action. It could just be that my swaying had calmed. The concept of being able to balance on one leg for a couple of seconds made all the difference for me. My weight shift onto the standing leg was stronger, the damaged part of my brain had eased from bouncing about, my stumble from one leg balance had shifted away from me falling in the direction of the standing leg, and I was stumbling more as if I had just become off balance.

Diary Entry - June 2022

Imagine the cerebellum filled with water and a magnetic rod in the centre with a ball attached to the rod by the magnetic force. Now and again, the magnetic rod loses power, and the attached ball tries to resurface, moving towards the edge of the cerebellum. Before it reaches its destination, the rod returns to power, and the magnetic force draws the ball back to the rod. Imagine this process in a continual loop, which is how my brain feels daily.

I would only leave my home with people I knew who understood my unpredictable actions from time to time. I had to trust them to help me if required. No one wants a mishap to happen, and I would always leave my home with the outlook that 'I'm strong enough mentally to control it'; though there was no overriding the brain, I learnt that. If it wanted me to fail, it would win, no matter how much I talked to it. Nothing was strong enough to override the brain's chain of thought.

After three years, it was more prominent that all my actions were controlled and dictated by the injured section of my brain.

My brain judder prominently occurs when I place my left foot on the ground. The type of brain judder I experience depends on the terrain I'm walking on.

My brain sometimes revolved around a gravity wheel sensation while walking. For example, I would walk along a pavement, and when I reached the end, I had to go either left or right. Now, I wanted the action to be as fluid as possible, so on reaching the end of the pavement and turning in whichever direction, I stopped at the end and turned my body first before walking. With the turning sensation, the brain goes into its gravity wheel sensation, making the turning action quite overpowering, which causes me to make incorrect steps with the force of my brain pulling me outwards. So, if I'm turning right on the pavement, my brain has a powerful pull left, so I must be careful with my steps. If the pavement leads straight onto a road, the brain pull can see me step off the pavement and onto the road; even with being link-armed with someone, this effect still takes place.

6 - Bladder and bowel

Upon coming home, I occasionally wet the bed at night. It wasn't frequent, though it did happen. I would dream I was having a wee and actually have one. It's quite ironic when I never usually dream, so when I did have a wee episode, I would wake as I somehow knew it wasn't correct. This lasted about three years after the bleed, and then it stopped. I used to think it was because I had a catheter for a couple of months. Still, the longer it continued, the more I researched the situation. It turned out to be a post-stroke/brain haemorrhage symptom of incontinence. I was just fortunate I didn't have daytime concerns. I used a waterproof bed protector and waterproof bed sheets, which I could easily place under my bed sheet if I were sleeping away from home.

Also, my bowel movement changed. I never went to the toilet how I used to pre-AVM bleed. It was almost as if the brain had forgotten how to, and I continually struggled. I tried to get advice from the doctor and received some input from a pelvic floor physio. It didn't completely solve the issues, but it helped. They taught me the correct way to go to the toilet, but I was left wondering if it was due to the damage caused to the brain.

One thing I did try was cutting out caffeine. I went decaf. This helped my concerns. It wasn't the solution, but it did aid a positive response.

7 - Inner sway, spring-like moments

Within the first year, I experienced a couple of spring-like sensations. My skeleton would turn into a human spring and bounce me all over the place. One example I remember is when I walked across my lounge, which didn't involve too many steps, and there was a footstool to the side. I was looking forward towards the sofa where I wanted to sit. My brain thought it didn't want to bash into the footstool on passing, and out of the corner of my eye, I could see the footstool. Due to not being able to multitask all the required needs, my brain would go into a frenzy, placing my body into a spring-like motion. I'd see myself falling forward onto the footstool and then going into a bouncing mess where the brain could not process all the information at once. This happened on more than one occasion. On other occasions, I would see the brain switch off, just like someone had flicked a switch off, enabling it to no longer work. This was a familiar occurrence during the first couple of years post-bleed. The spring-like sensations eased away, though the inner body sway remained.

You know the concept of a jack-in-the-box, where a doll-like object is at the end of a secure spring at the bottom. You can push the doll in any direction, and it will spring back and forth until the motion runs out of power - that was exactly how my skeleton felt. I would call it my inner sway. No one could see me swaying on the outside, though, on the inside, I was viciously swaying and bouncing at times, usually back and forth. This was a symptom which I carried for years post-bleed; it may even be a symptom which never goes away. It has calmed down over the years, so there is hope it may disperse. I have adapted my abilities, which incorporate the sway. Although I'm aware it's occurring, I seem to get on with my task in action, and the task slowly overrides the swaying. Sometimes, it would feel like my feet were tied together and anchored at the bottom of the ocean - swaying from my feet in the sea's current. This was such a bizarre, disheartening sensation as I would wish to be still.

Diary Entry - January 2020

I was taken to a nearby city in early 2020 using Park and Ride; I was getting better at being a passenger using Park and Ride and using a bus. I noticed that I was not swaying as much when stopping in shops as I used to. I attempted a few walking steps outside shops and within crowds, which I would not have tried on previous visits.

Diary Entry - February 2021

Vibrations were sent down my left side from head to heel. Still, over time, it moulded into a rod sensation. I had a rod from my head to my heel on my left side. I noticed how the rod sensation had eased down to mainly my left leg. I no longer had the sensation from my head to my waist on my left.

Treadmill memories:

In my first year of using the treadmill, I swayed side to side quite a bit, so I practised one-handed to strengthen the sway. I would have to tell the left leg to move physically; sometimes, I would get stuck and not step forward. After around a year, the left foot started to feel more at ease, as it felt like all the weight was on the outside of the foot. This was all I could feel, which was very uncomfortable - it was like walking on an edge.

I would follow a companion, be it family or a friend, around the store while shopping, and it may involve stop-start reactions. This would prove extremely difficult for me as my internal swaying skeleton would wish to continue walking forward, and my brain would say stop. This caused my calf muscles to want to pop out as they were being used to stop me from continuing my forward journey; they endured a lot of strain.

When getting out of a car, I would shake internally quite severely. I'd have to wait for my accompanying individual to assist me during the visit to wherever that may have been. This was the case for a good three years. Only after this time did I start to acknowledge I was shaking less. If we were parking in a flat car park and going to a store, I was becoming more able to do it on my own accord, provided we were parked close to the store. I would not have dreamed it would have taken this length of time to achieve. I started believing improvement was coming to light after the three-year window.

8 - My left

Being bashful was quite upsetting. Taking out my left side from time to time due to not reacting quickly enough to protect myself from this happening was becoming painful. Let's just say I didn't know my own strength. I'm surprised I never had bruises up my left arm or leg, as the number of things I had bashed into over time could quite easily have done this to me. The number of times I walked into the wall on my left or even door frames, pillars, or anything on my left that drew me in. I would bash myself continually; yes, it was frustrating and often hurt. I would just continue to remind myself that this situation wasn't forever. Well, so I hoped anyway. I was confident in my body's repair. Six years on from my bleed, this situation did improve even though it took all this time to do so, and even then, it still happened. I had to keep my smile going and laugh at the awkward scenarios I encountered. I was sometimes quite weak at controlling my left side; I would aim for a left wall pillar, for example, and would think I needed to shift my weight to avoid this from happening, and yet the brain was so heavy and weighted to the left, it would override anything which I was trying to achieve. Sometimes, I just wanted to cry - who could live a life like this? I would have these moments and then talk myself out of them. I would always tell myself it was part of the healing process.

The left side of my body didn't register for a few years, and I encountered my fair share of walking blunders. I'd walk into obstacles in my path, down a corridor, and into the wall on my left side. I would walk into anything on my left. It was like my brain saw it but would never react to it. Sometimes it was almost like my brain switched off. My left side was severely affected, and I continued to treat it as I always would have, in the hope it would eventually ease away. I hoped that my repetitive actions would become the norm. Sometimes, I would see the obstacle in my path and not avoid it as my processing of the signal was super slow, which prevented me from acting upon avoiding the obstacle. I had to make the mistake of walking into obstacles in my path so I could map out pathways within my brain to prevent it from happening in the future.

It took around two years before I could leave the dinner table without bashing my left arm when getting up, as this action would freak the brain out quite a bit. Also, getting out of the car after three years was becoming less challenging. I had to learn a new technique for my balance that would prevent me from feeling as though I wanted to fall. It was nearly three years before I could walk through a doorway without touching it to judge its width and to steady me through.

On occasion, when using stairs, I would purposely use my left side for the handrail. My left arm never liked being used, so I would force it and mentally prepare myself for not having a right side. It was extremely difficult, as the palm of my hand would clam up, becoming rather sweaty, making sliding along a handrail rather difficult. It was apparent to the brain that my left side was no longer running automatically. I always must move my left limbs manually. The vision from my left eye is slightly uncomfortable, if you could even imagine a sensation from sight. Every time the left foot hits the ground, it sends a judder to the brain.

I used to always talk to my left foot and leg to move. I would count it in on a 1, 2 system. If I acknowledged my left leg with my brain, it made me walk straighter. I was less inclined to stagger right by overcompensating on my right leg, which resulted in hurting my right calf.

I struggled a lot with my left arm. I would quite often see my left arm juddering randomly. I had very little control over it. I couldn't pick things up with my left hand to eat or drink and was solely right-hand dependent.

I couldn't use my left arm for over a year as it was very unpredictable with its movements. It was known to viciously shake uncontrollably. I couldn't hold anything in my left hand, such as vitamins/tablets, to pass a piece of paper or object to someone or to use my left hand as the dominant party. Even though this had calmed down over time, it was still a concern after two years.

By the end of 2019, I slowly started to recognise my left side. In early 2020, I started new exercises to help strengthen my left, which involved pushing hard down on my left heel, hopping and jumping whilst holding onto a worktop, lifting a light dumbbell, standing on one leg against a wall, and heel raises to strengthen the calf, to name a few. I was confident these exercises would eventually have the left naturally recognised by the brain.

As I walked about during the day, my left leg was disconnected from my brain. It had a particularly unusual sensation. I had to talk to the leg to help it move and lift; otherwise, I would kick the ground continually. I had a rod sensation, which ran from my head to my heel on my left. It was an internal sensation and couldn't be seen by any onlooker, and no actual rod was involved. It swayed back and forth. If I wanted to do any balancing which was weight bearing on my left, I would judder. My brain would only blackout on the left, and I would spin to the left.

During my fourth year, 2021, my left side was prominent in the damaged side of the body; I'd continue with a rod-like sensation running from my skull to my foot or have an elastic band pulled tight sensation with an added loose swaying feeling. With the rod sensation, I felt a rigid sway. Have you ever tried placing a bend in a steel rod? That is all I can think of with this. Well, that was me wishing to bend my left knee whilst walking.

A heavy, weighted rod ran through my left side from head to heel. It was usually the top of this that would try to pull me forward. If I was looking ahead and then down, I would be attracted to falling forward. If I was leaning forward and moving my eyes to look down, I would have to reach forward with my hands to steady myself. It was a particularly bizarre sensation, along with many others, which makes it hard to describe any of it.

I was in my fifth year of recovery, and I noticed how problematic my left leg was. I felt it was always problematic though I felt as many symptoms had calmed down the left leg was highlighted in its hindrance behaviour. It was very good at dictating my walking pattern. The bones in the leg would go into their rod-like sensation and pull me forward. It was hard to lift when tired and when weight bearing this leg made the leg offer very little support. The left knee was seen to judder making it extremely hard to push weight through the left leg. It was very good at making me move in the left direction; it had its own mind.

My left foot didn't like the attention and limelight. If I were to weight bear it or lift it to perform a balance exercise, my brain would struggle to keep it steady. It didn't like work; pretty much like most of the human race, we all wish to grow a money tree and drink our desired drink with either the beach, mountain or open landscape at the bottom of our garden and live a hassle-free life. Then we wake up and, don our work attire and live another working day. I'm sure everyone has, at some point, had the desired dream.

Where was I? Apart from going off topic, the heavyweight that stemmed from the cerebellum would judder backwards if I required it to work. This resulted in me going backwards with the judder. Upsetting and frustrating would always come to mind. If I was at the bottom of a flight of stairs I wanted to go up, I would look up to see if the coast was clear, and looking up would send the brain into its judder. I was helped to practice stepping sideways and backward, which should be natural. Here I am, struggling to keep balance to perform such a simple action. It was now down to me being pulled backwards with the judder sensation that I would acknowledge how important it was to know and understand how to step backward. It's especially challenging if the judder takes place unexpectedly and you're standing on a slope. It all starts to become interesting.

Diary Entries - February 2021

My left head-to-heel rod sensation is easing. The left foot edge is becoming less noticeable and prominent in my chain of thought.

The brain realised that my left side was very heavy in sensation. When stepping forward, my left leg would wish to throw me forward.

Diary Entries - April 2021

My left leg was known for its constant judder. It was around four years when it eased down. I could make my few steps not to be awarded a juddering left leg; I could step out of the vehicle after a drive and stand with the ease of the judder. It would be actions we don't even think twice about, and I was now super appreciative that I could achieve them again. However, on occasion, this wasn't always the case. Most days, my left leg simply doesn't want to know. I send it commands, and it chooses to ignore me, making it difficult to lift.

My left leg offered very little support when practising exercises requiring leading with the left leg, which proved very difficult. If I were side-stepping, leading with my left, I would be balancing on a rod when drawing my right foot in to join my left. I encountered no concerns when doing the same action, leading with my right. If I used my left hand for the handrail, it would clam up and go sweaty, making it extremely hard to slide along the rail.

Sometimes, it's just a case of moving my left leg, which consumes most of my energy. When walking, my left side doesn't automatically move; I manually move it. I must talk through the actions to perform them. This alone consumes my strength and energy. The left side of my brain becomes numb, and my left leg becomes super heavy and feels unnatural.

During my fourth-year post-bleed, I started to try to have my left side recognised by my brain. I concentrated on using the left-hand rail, for example, over the right, using my left arm to link arms with people opposed to my right. I basically had to make my right side invisible. It was hard and uncomfortable.

Even though I struggled with my left leg, it continually improved. It was hard to acknowledge any improvement as the leg would be so uncomfortable, though it was happening. Lifting the leg was one of its priority concerns. It was hard lifting my leg to walk, and at times, I would walk and forget to lift it as I always had to do this manually. This would always, as expected, result in a stumble of sorts, which I would have to laugh off. It's a good job I had good laughter muscles as I used them a lot.

Diary Entries - July 2021

I am trying to improve my left arm by doing dumbbell exercises most days. My left leg was still particularly slow with reactions. At times, it was hard to lift, an action that onlookers could not see. The signal from my leg to my brain was clearly damaged. Repairing it was super hard, and then I would take steps and have to rely on the leg. Sometimes, I would stumble to the left as my brain felt like it had switched off.

My left calf feels worked. This is the first time my right calf feels fine, apart from wishing to explode from my leg. My left side appears more noticeable with its deficits. The leg stops communicating, and my arm doesn't like to be relied upon.

My left leg was seen to offer little support when standing. When I tried to walk from standing, it would give on me, which resulted in me saving myself from falling. It was very good at juddering from the knee; this was visual, and others could see it. I'd want to weight bear on my left, and the judder would make it quite unbearable. When walking, my left foot often felt like it was round, almost like it was the shape of a football. This made walking quite uncomfortable as my foot continually wanted to roll outwards, giving me a wide gait to the left.

I often practised placing pants on whilst standing. A daily action we all do only now had been taken away from me, so I practised hard to regain it. I could stand on my right leg for seconds while placing my left leg through the trousers opening, though I couldn't do this while my left leg stood. After three years of continually doing this daily, the leg slowly offered support. I no longer wished to topple straight over when I lifted the right leg to place it through the trousers opening. It was feeling stronger in its stance.

Diary Entries - December 2021

I feel like my brain's left side is in constant fog. My vision from my left eye is still a problem, and any thought process I try to generate from my left hurts.

My left side is particularly poor. My vision isn't correct through the left eye; it hurts, and the left side of my brain is struggling. My left leg and knee are weak, and I'm struggling with the signal from brain to leg. Lifting my left leg hurts the left side of my brain. The left eye wishes to continually close, and it's straining with its vision.

I'm still contending with a heavy weight on the left side of my brain sensation, which seems always to move about.

Tying bras and bikini tops up was difficult due to my left arm; I struggled to hold the left strap. Regarding bottoms, I changed from wearing trousers with zips and buttons to those with an elasticated waist.

In 2023, I got an FES device on the NHS to help my left leg lift. They are designed to help foot drop though I had multiple troubles with the leg in general and it was an experiment to see if it helped. The quick answer was that it did help.

The leg became lighter to lift when in use. I noticed that I was becoming super tired. I pieced the jigsaw together and concluded that the device was wearing my brain out. Due to all the tasks it was performing and the constant vibrations it offered to stimulate the muscles, my brain was tired of it. It didn't discourage me from using it, as it offered such positive feedback. Becoming tired was the sacrifice to help aid my left leg, which was an okay deal.

When I was nearly seven years post-bleed, I decided to investigate my left foot rolling outwards, generated from my ankle area. I had struggled with this for some years, and it was usually highlighted by the brain pulling me to the left. My chain of thought was that if someone placed a wedge under my foot in that area, it may discourage the roll outwards and remind the brain not to do this. I spoke to my doctor, who referred me to podiatry. At my appointment, I discovered this was a known procedure they did under an insole to help balance the foot out. I was a little disappointed that it had taken nearly seven years for this conversation and for them to make this suggestion. How proactive the suggestion was, was going to be a work in progress.

At the end of the appointment, I asked whether they could see a difference in my foot.

To which they replied, "You have foot drop."

Foot drop? Not one person had made this observation of all the physios I had seen over the years. I was so disappointed with them all. It was only brought to my attention because I asked the question. Yes, I asked the question. At least now I could work towards helping it. Luckily, I had been working with an FES device to help the left leg for other reasons, so I had the equipment. I made a future appointment as a follow-up, and I was going to look at suggested footwear that would help with this symptom. It may not be the most attractive attire, but if it helps, I don't care. After all, I felt like the performing monkey, so I may as well dress like one.

9 - Fatigue

I found that after two and a half years, I was becoming more tired and requiring days off from doing anything. These days away from activities did give me a boost for when I next attempted them. Tiredness was a game changer. During year five, I was forever tired. I was exhausted from all the effort I had been putting into my recovery and from continually trying to improve myself. This tiredness just showed me how much I was in denial of the brain haemorrhage happening to me in my early days of recovery. I was so convinced I would get me back that I bypassed any episodes of tiredness. During year five of recovery and how I was still not independent, took its toll. My most restful setting was sitting on my bed with no TV or radio, in complete silence. This was my heaven. I would sit and stare out the window. I enjoyed this so much because I wasn't struggling; I wasn't trying to go about my day in my new manner of awkwardness. Instead, I was sitting effortlessly, feeling content.

Reading my notes was quite motivational. They highlighted how far I had come in my recovery and had achieved, which made me smile.

My fifth year was my hardest to date, and I little knew at this stage that the following years would prove just as challenging regarding fatigue. I was always tired, and my mood was low. The length of recovery wore me out, and my right leg was constantly painful. I became quite inactive as everything I wanted to do was such hard work. The right leg calf pain was at the top of the Richter scale, so I was more inactive as I didn't want to use the leg.

I learned to acknowledge how hard it was to achieve simple tasks and accept that I needed to sit it out. Unless I wanted to feel at my worst with tiredness for trying to carry out the task! I stayed behind at home more and said no to days out which was very unlike me. An afternoon spent at the beach, or an afternoon spent in the garden? I would choose the garden as it was the easiest option. I didn't have to make an effort to go down the steps to the nearest beach, which offered a juddery handrail for support. Then, link-arm walk across the beach, dodging people seated in their position for the day, to find a spot to sit, on a slight decline just before it entered the water.

During my sixth-year post-bleed, I attended groups put together for people with sight or symptom concerns. I would look really worn out and fatigued afterwards, and the classes only ran for a couple of hours each week. It would take me the following two days to rebuild my strength, which worried me as I realised that I really was struggling.

I often spoke of giving myself complete rest days - a day of grace from exercises. Well, that was the intention anyway. It was very rare I rewarded myself a day completely free from doing anything. I'd have a rest day yet still go on my sit-up device, practice the stairs, assisted jumping on the spot, step in and out of the kitchen into the garden, which involved a step and some days I'd venture onto my balance board, and so on. All I was giving myself a rest day from was going outside for assisted walking practice. I found it hard to do nothing. Knowing I wasn't expecting to go outside gave my brain a rest from preparing for the venture. As the years passed and the fatigue grew, I eventually gave in to a complete rest day.

10 - Menstrual cycle

No one ever comments on the menstrual cycle. It's common knowledge that we women go through this cycle for most of our lives, so it's only right that I share the following information. As we are aware, our brains control our bodies. After my second bleed, I never had a cycle for four months. I have no idea why, only that my brain had experienced a severe bleed, which caused damage to the affected area. When the cycle started again, it was never the same cycle and flow as before. I also experienced multiple symptoms a week before and a week after the event that would usually reflect my current symptoms; only it would heighten specific symptoms in my weak areas. Like my shaking would be more frequent and I'd be extremely weak with it. My left leg would judder a lot more, and my knee would buckle easily. My left arm judder would appear more frequently. Occasionally, I would get cold sores on my lips or nose.

11 – Spinning

I was often asked if I suffer with vertigo or constant spinning within the brain. I had never had vertigo, so I was unfamiliar with this experience, but I didn't have a spinning sensation in my brain, nor did I feel dizzy or nauseous. When I thought about this a year later, it occurred to me that maybe I was misinterpreting the sensation or that what I had been experiencing was the sensation to which the doctors were referring. To this day I still don't know. I guess everyone interprets the feeling differently. I would get a 'Russian doll effect' within the brain's injured part, the cerebellum. I would describe my spinning sensation as a ball within a ball inside the cerebellum section of the brain. The smallest inner ball was the ball which was spinning. I received a referred sensation to this motion.

I had no understanding of what was happening, and I'm guessing no one ever will. It's all assumptions, and as we are all built differently, we will never have a pinpoint. Still, I could be completely incorrect in thinking this. The way we are moving forward with science, who knows what discoveries there will be in the future. The spinning sensation would create quite a pull, and as the months went on, the pull lessened, though the sensation still occurred. It never actually went away, even when lying still with my eyes closed. At six years post-bleed, I was still incurring this sensation; it would heighten when tired.

12 - Sleeping

When I first came home in 2017 from my second bleed, I had developed a new sleep pattern. I basically never slept in the day, no matter how tired I appeared to be and the fatigue I would undergo. It was extremely frustrating. I would go to sleep between 10 - 11 pm and wake consistently between 1.30 - 2.30 am for the bathroom. It was like my brain only knew how to shut down for three hours, so to wake up at 4 - 5 am was truly amazing. It was probably during 2020 that I started sleeping episodes where I would sleep slightly longer throughout the night. The episodes only lasted a few days, though it was good enough for me that they even happened. I hoped that, in time, my sleep pattern would alter again. I never had dreams post-bleed, as there were no nighttime activities within my brain. It was like I had literally been switched off. I did miss this, and it was strange never to dream after years and years of having dreams.

I attempted many approaches to going to bed in the hope that they would help me sleep longer, none of which had an effect. These included early nights - I'm talking 9 - 10 pm, no caffeine after 2 pm, no fluid after 7 pm, herbal sleeping drinks, vitamins, exercise, and sometimes trying to stay up later.

I have done some research and discovered that this is quite common after a stroke/brain haemorrhage to only sleep for short bursts at a time. It seems you either lean towards sleeping quite easily, so anytime or cannot sleep easily, which is me.

13 - Multitask

I couldn't multitask my actions. A good example of this is walking. I'm required to see where I'm going and move my legs to walk, be on sound alert for traffic and other walkers, move my arms, balance, and move my head. How good or bad the lighting is had an effect, to list a few. I was unable to perform this task.

Symptom notes - October 2019

-Getting out of the car is starting to improve

-Standing in general, my posture has become much stronger

-Getting better at walking stairs with handrail

-Weight in my head is easing

-Body becoming less dead weight

-Very hard to walk and look at something; it was not possible but it has started to improve. It does throw my walking out

-I pull intense facial expressions by concentrating so much on my walking. Starting to ease up

-My brain becomes extremely tired, and it's when this happens that I tend just to want to topple over, not that toppling has happened as I try my hardest to overcome it

-In the evenings, I sway more and become unsteady. I guess everyone becomes fatigued and tired in evenings. My body shuts down. It's like it's dealing with alcohol but hasn't had any. On the odd occasion that I meet friends and have one drink, it affects my body as if it had five - my inner sway increases. The simple answer is to simply not have an alcoholic drink

-I still have the spring sensation. My feet are solid on the ground, but you are like a spring from the feet up. Jack in the box comes to mind

-When on the treadmill, if I think of something other than walking, my feet stop working and freeze. I must bring my concentration back onto walking. If I never reacted quickly enough, I would go backwards

-It felt as though my legs couldn't temperature control. They were always super warm from the knee down

-I had intense discomfort behind the right knee

-I remember (going back a year) that I would lie on my bed to relax, and my body wouldn't stop bouncing within. It always reminded me of a flicked elastic band. I would cry internally as there was no escape from my symptoms. All I could do was tell myself it wasn't forever and only temporary. I did not fully know if this was true, but it was all I could do for myself

-Swaying internally lessened around November 2019

-For the entire of 2019, the left side of my body was alien, the left side sways internally constantly

Diary Entries - January 2020

I noticed that my swaying when walking with another has calmed down quite a bit. My standing has become stronger. I'm noticing how much good resting does for the body. Due to not sleeping during the day, doing nothing was beneficial.

I used to take multiple vitamins as I felt the body required them after the trauma it had endured. I'm not convinced taking vitamins helped my recovery, but I'm sure they did it no harm. Our bodies are unique to us, and we all require individual assistance with our requirements. Just because I felt they were of no help does not mean they will not have any assistance to you. My body could have been of reasonable levels of the supplements, so I felt no effects from them; someone else's body may be deprived of a particular vitamin and require it. I am no medical professional, so I cannot judge this.

*"Life is not about waiting for the storm to pass;
it's about learning to dance in the rain."*

Vivian Greene

Chapter Four

It's All Just a Balancing Act/ Recalibrate

When I refer to balance, I'm not referring to how you balance your life concerning work, diet, and exercise. I'm referring to it in terms of the body being in a balanced proportion to stand and taking steps, turning, moving an arm, etc. I was only too familiar with how the structure of the skeleton balanced bone on bone. There is so much we do that requires balance, and we are unaware of it. It's only from being stripped of my balance that I noticed how much I do, which requires a balanced core.

I remember when it felt to me like my spine was disconnected from my pelvis in my early stages. It was beyond loose and moved only too freely in any direction. It took a good two years to become steadier in itself. At the time, I would be thinking to myself, will this improve?

It took until around December 2020 when my mind started to forget how easily I used to balance my body. For over three years, I had only now acknowledged that I'd forgotten the ease of this action as it was previously automatic. I was only aware of the challenge this action involved due to my daily living.

Without my core strength, which gives you balance, I was unable to achieve the simplest of tasks - tasks we all do automatically, like having a cuppa while sitting in bed. Now, I couldn't sit up in bed as I would just flop to the side.

Without my balance, I was also unable to sit on the toilet, something you wouldn't even think of. I had a toilet frame to help me with this, which offered me support and confidence that I wasn't just going to wobble off. I had a grab rail placed in the shower, so I had something to hold and keep me steady while I showered.

I had sensations linking muscles and bones, and I was learning their relationships. I learned how important balancing on one leg was towards the body. Something to this day I still cannot achieve. We hugely require it for walking, as the grounded foot balances you when you step forward. I couldn't balance, so taking any form of step was challenging. Taking a large step was impossible. This results in balancing for longer on the grounded foot as you step further away.

Balancing exercises were something I would do daily. Type rope balancing was the most challenging for me, and it took up all my energy. Type rope standing consisted of balancing one foot in front of the other, so the toe heel, and I'm still trying to achieve it. It took me a year of doing it every day to manage five seconds without holding on, and even then, I couldn't position my feet in front of one another. I would have a golf ball sensation or something similar in my brain's damaged area. It would pull me to the side when placing either foot out in front of the other, and I would have to fight it so that I didn't give in to it. I would tell myself that I had to override it and concentrate on stabilising my feet by spreading the weight throughout the entire foot.

To begin with, when I started practising this action, I would stand with my feet slightly apart instead of directly in front of one another. Over time, I shrunk the distance between my feet, so they were more or less in front of one another. Even at four years, I could still not achieve this action when I positioned them directly in front of one another. Every muscle in the leg placed behind would be working in the calf. I had a sore right calf, and when I placed the right leg behind this leg, it felt like it wanted to burst and hurt so much. I wouldn't even be weight-bearing on it, strangely.

During 2020, I started practising balancing on one leg, as this was non-existent. I'd do this while standing against a wall. If I raised my right leg, I would stand, and my weight would often shift from the front of my foot to the heel. There was no balance spot. Or I'd notice that all my weight was through the front of my foot. I would then readjust, and all my weight would only go to the heel of my foot. I was like a rocking chair in motion, and my brain didn't know what to do with it and would judder because of being confused.

I used to stand on one leg easily before my bleed, but now I struggle to form any balance and achieve it by holding on. Where have those days gone? I knew I would get it back with time, but I had to hold a particular type of patience.

When balancing on one leg, I feel all my muscles working to keep me balanced and feel all the strains on the ankle and knee joints. After a year and a half of practising this action, bearing in mind I still couldn't achieve five seconds on any one leg after this length of time, this one particular day when practising the action, I didn't acknowledge all the sensations involved, I just attempted the action. This, to me, was hope that long-awaited improvement was coming. I wasn't achieving a longer balance yet, though I was experiencing a natural sensation-free experience. I knew this new sensation would be a one-off experience. Still, this one-off experience was enough to encourage me to believe that improvements would happen.

Practising the stairs at home, which certainly required balance, had an advantage with narrow steps and walls on either side. However, sometimes, it was a disadvantage because they didn't have much space. The back of my brain would judder uncontrollably when practising stairs as I was making my left side work. Around the three-year mark, I noticed my brain was getting less freaked out. I could still not easily achieve the stairs using the handrail, though contributing factors had calmed down.

The stages I would perform whilst putting on bottoms were first to have a mindset that involved huge amounts of concentration before attempting any actions. Then, I had to wait for the brain to calm down and be still so that the action could take place. If the brain couldn't calm completely, I had to time my actions between the juddering of the brain. This usually takes a few minutes.

Stage 1: Lifting the foot off the floor to place it through the trouser/bottoms opening for that leg. As soon as the foot is lifted, I topple over. For me, it's natural to place my right leg through the trouser opening first. This only resulted in me toppling over every time. I then switched it to my left foot being used first. I had to switch the action and start with my left leg. For some bizarre reason, this worked better for me.

Stage 2: If my foot caught any trouser openings, it would confuse the brain and send it into judder overdrive. This would result in me stopping the action and resorting to sitting down or lying to complete the action. Once the brain was stressed, it would not let me attempt any action.

Stage 3: Placing the foot through the opening was completed extremely quickly due to balance. I would thump the floor when the foot was through the opening for support in my balance.

Stage 4: It occurred to me that after around eight months of practising this action, I required my brain to multitask to complete it. It had to balance on one leg whilst lifting the opposite leg to place through the trouser opening; with this action, a forward step motion was taking place. Not every attempt at this action was productive. It took months and months to achieve. Despite how upsetting it was to attempt this action, knowing how difficult it was, I would do it every morning to get dressed and evening when going to bed.

After three years of practising, I was still struggling with the action, my main improvement being I didn't have to rush it; I was managing to achieve this in a slower motion. Even after four years of daily practice, I still struggled with it. Certain aspects of the action had become easier, though I still couldn't easily complete the action. After five years, I calmed down with practising and started questioning myself: why did I put myself through stress? I could do the action sometimes depending on the bottoms, but I gave into it and started just sitting to place any bottoms on. Even this proved challenging because when I would lift the leg off the floor to place it through the bottom opening, it would pull me to the side of the lifted leg. Even being seated, I struggled with my balance.

I discovered balance within the feet plays a major part in our body's balance system. When you step onto and off a step, for example, how much weight shift goes on within your foot and leg goes unnoticed. When you step back - you place the foot down onto its tiptoes and then flatten the foot down in a rolling motion. While proceeding with this action, a major weight shift is happening. When you step backward, all the weight is at the toes first, and your weight shifts over the foot as you make the backward step. For me, whilst doing this action, you can be immensely pulled backwards by the brain. I feel that this was the reasoning behind my jack-in-a-box moments when stepping up onto the step in practice. My brain motion was moving forward, though once my step was complete, my brain motion was still moving me forward, though it was also trying to stop causing a counteracting motion. This would result in my spring-like motions of moving back and forth. I was always amazed at how I hadn't been catapulted forward and caused myself injury.

Diary Entries - 22/11/20

Balancing - It took me one year of practising on one leg to conclude that I could balance competently on one leg for three seconds. When I wished to rely on it for balance, the leg would feel uncomfortable from the knee down. It would become extremely rigid on the outside of the lower leg. It was very uncomfortable and unnatural.

My right leg, where I was putting down all sensations to overcompensating, was super heavy in my early stages. This sensation returned after three years post-bleed. I was hoping for all sensations experienced to ease away, though this one had returned completely, and I hoped it would be one last visit before saying goodbye.

An example of how balance has improved is when I put my socks on whilst leaning against my bed. I would stand with my back against the bed and lift the foot up on which I placed the sock. When my left leg was the supporting leg for me to place a sock on my right foot, it would be super weak, and I would fall over to the left as the leg would offer no support. After four and a half years, the leg had become stronger and supported the leaning position, enabling me to place my right sock on. I was no longer toppling over to the left every time, just on occasion.

"Life's too short not to laugh and joke along the way."

Unknown

Chapter Five | Walk the Line

The chapter title is quite ironic, as I could not walk on a line. My gait was wide, and attempting a narrower gait was impossible in the early years due to my balance, though this never stopped me from trying. I had a goal to achieve this action; I just knew it would take some time. No able individual will ever understand the hardship and awkwardness of learning to walk. It's a unique journey for the individual who is experiencing it.

In my early days of recovery, I was unable to walk two steps; I wasn't even able to stand. I was literally a limp, shaking mess. I started home recovery with my Dad's help on a Zimmer frame, which I replaced with a four-wheeled walker. I then preferred to walk only, assisted by another individual, as I found using another person was more supportive of my circumstances. I had zero balance, and the weight of my brain controlled my movements. Due to my poor balance, walking aids only hindered me. I could not think about the equipment and the terrain and consider the steps I needed to take simultaneously. I had basically lost the ability to multitask.

The remainder of 2017 didn't see me do much in the way of rehab, as I was too unsteady and floppy and unable to stand with ease. I would shake uncontrollably. The start of 2018 saw me and my Dad working on my rehab. I'd perform daily exercises to help build my muscle strength back up. Also, the common saying was that repetitive exercise was good for recovery as you're rebuilding pathways. Another action I would take was walking across my kitchen floor, which was only eight steps but plenty for me. Dad would count 'one, two', and I would walk to the count.

Numbering my legs told me which leg to move. My left leg liked to step wide, which made me feel unbalanced. Another kitchen exercise was sideways stepping, holding onto the worktop. My left leg didn't like lifting and was very clunky with knee movement. It was very hard to perform this movement with the left leg leading. Sideways stepping is beneficial in everyday life, more so than you realise. For example, I'd walk across my bedroom, and if I had a blanket thrown on the floor, I couldn't walk over it as it would send me into a bounce from my knees, so I had to step around it. Now, to do this, I sidestep. This is when I realised how beneficial the sidestep would be for me. I practised this daily. I'd also shake quite vigorously when holding on. Nothing was easy. Sometimes, Dad would clear the driveway of cars so I could walk a few steps without assistance. This was very challenging for me; walking felt super uncomfortable, so I imagine it looked like it.

Walking was extremely hard for me. There were many days where I simply did not want to perform this action. Though it was the story that if I didn't use my legs, I would lose it, this saying is completely correct. The longer I went with little attempted walking, the harder it was for me when I wanted to walk a little further as the pain I would encounter was intense. I believe many people, given my circumstances, give up trying to walk and accept a wheelchair. This wasn't me. I wanted to walk, even if it was only a few steps. I needed to walk for my independence, which proved a small snippet. No one understood that any form of walking aid was of no help to my situation. It could be a specialist, friend or family member suggesting the aid; I would always explain why the brain couldn't currently multitask and why it was more a hindrance than a helpful piece of equipment. It was always taken onboard as a surprise. If anything, it would likely see me fall over than help with my balance. Thinking of anything more than actual walking would be too much for my brain to digest. The pull within the brain was so powerful that nothing could help to stop me from toppling to the side.

Occasionally, I'd get stuck when I attempted walking independently, resulting in only a few steps. For example, I would hit a slight decline underfoot whilst walking in a straight line and running sideways across that line, creating a decline. I'd continuously walk on the decline, making me walk sideways until I spun around to face the decline's downward view. Sometimes, it could be dangerous as the slight decline underfoot could bore me into a road, hedge, cliff top, etc.

The beach was very beneficial in aiding my assisted walking. However, I felt I was on a catwalk with everyone watching when, in fact, no one was probably watching. Try telling the brain that. I couldn't focus on anyone, which probably went in my favour, so I learnt to just ignore people.

My legs would not hold any strength when entering or leaving the sea. It's like they couldn't support me and hold me up tall. I have tried strengthening my legs at the gym with no avail. My left leg, or stroke leg as I'd refer to it, would quite often get stuck during movement. It would stop working, and I would have to wait for it to wake again. This was a little disheartening for me and a little frustrating for my company, which was assisting me.

My legs were a problem for me after my induced coma. They never felt connected to my body. I had severe temperature control problems with them in the hospital. My legs took a long time to be recognised by my brain. Each leg had its concerns, making attempted walking extremely difficult. My left leg offered very little support; at times, it was like I never even had a left leg. As well as the other symptoms I've previously described, it would freeze up and pull me over to the left, resulting in me walking into whatever was in my path. My brain received the minimal assisted walking I did during the first two years as very mechanical. All my joints were bolted together, and it was very uncomfortable. I also had to continually talk to the leg for it to move. For example, if I stumped my leg, it would be due to not seeing correctly; it would panic my brain, sending multiple signals that would freak my body out.

My right leg offered an uncomfortable calf muscle. Even at six years post-bleed, I still struggled with the calf pain which had been there for years. I was unable to weight bear the leg without it being really painful. I saw numerous individuals for advice on this, but I struggled to find anyone who could help with the pain. It felt like my brain only recognised my right leg, which resulted in there being severe pain behind the right knee, on the back of the leg, not within the knee. I received a lot of pain in my right upper calf; I could feel what felt like all the muscle fibres pulled tight; this started off behind my right knee at the back of the leg, where I imagined the ligaments were. Two years post-bleed, the tendons or muscle behind the right knee became extremely sore on extension. I believed it was down to the leg compensating for the left leg. It took over two years before I started getting feelings in my left leg again. I thought my right leg knee pain would ease up at this time, but it never did. I felt the leg muscles had moulded to a manner to support the left side due to overcompensating, and now, I had to remould to uncompensate.

When my right calf was manipulated, it became extremely aggravated resulting in more pain. I tried various painkillers over the years, though none of them helped. It was almost like the body was now bypassing any relief that a painkiller would offer. I tried massage and then dry needling, which only aggravated it. I tried topical creams and balms with no effect; I tried a tens machine, which again offered no relief. I did a lot of weight-bearing on my left leg to help ease the pain from the right leg, but it made no difference.

I tried strengthening the left leg at the gym, but targeting it for exercise only annoyed it and it would go into its rod sensation. It also offered no relief towards my right leg. I was at a complete standstill.

I tried a patella strap, which helped, but it really hurt when I removed it. I rubbed muscle creams into the calf and behind the right knee, which did nothing, but I did receive a nice little massage in doing so, which can't be a bad thing.

I have had physios look at my right leg in all areas, but they have been unable to pinpoint any concerns. I have seen doctors who have also concluded the same. I had an ultrasound done, and it showed nothing. All of these are positive in that there is nothing to worry about. At the same time, it's frustrating as there is nothing to help heal or correct the pain, leaving me with discomfort and pain with no solution.

I tried using compression socks, though I felt these aggravated it as they retained the muscles in a position they didn't like. When I removed the socks, the muscles could spread out and relax, which released the pain caused by the muscles being kept in position. I tried calf stretches and Paracetamol, but nothing seemed to work. I believed I had done some muscle damage, and my efforts did not run deep enough to ease the concern. As my left leg became more recognised by the brain, it was only natural to think the right calf pain would ease up; I later learnt that this was wishful thinking.

During 2024, I had had enough of contending with this severe pain daily. I revisited the doctors who referred me to see the pain clinic. They put me forward for a nerve conduction study. This showed I had a mildly damaged nerve in my calf, which was causing all the pain. This is still ongoing, as I'm unsure if there is a solution for nerve damage.

I'd put a knee support on my left knee to help with its juddering, though this only helped keep the knee warm. Two years on, I started concentrating more on my left side. I would overbear on it to train the brain that I have a left side.

When I first came home in August 2017, I started not being able to stand for too long as my legs struggled to hold and support me. I would stand in front of the kitchen worktop and hold on, and I would practice letting go of it and standing without its support for ten seconds. Over time, I'd extend the length of time which I would stand for. It was only weeks before this moment that it would have been an automatic reaction to stand and look out the window without the holding on part.

Improving my standing action consumed all my energy. My legs instantly hurt upon standing, combined with keeping my balance. Now, to make such movements, I would have to think about the steps I must take: my arms should be moving, my eyesight had to be clear, my internal swaying had to be calm enough, my knees had to be strong, my brain had to be balanced and clearly thinking and not in a panicked frenzy, and lastly, I had to be aware of distractions (be it something in my path or noises).

My lower legs were most uncomfortable during the post-years from my bleeding. Walking in my early days was particularly painful. My balance relied on my lower legs, which would stop me in any rhythm and try to see me stumble or fall. They took the brunt of all my walking efforts.

They would ache with every standing action, the calves hurt, and at times, it felt very much like the muscles wanted to explode out of the legs after being jolted in all directions for balance purposes. The knees were also painful, and my feet had very little flex. The legs from the knees down had a sensation that I could only imagine to be like pulsating upon resting. Even upon waking, they would offer this sensation. It took a good couple of years to calm down, though it never dispersed, which was down to the balance not fully correcting. My lower legs remained super heavy and achy the first few years, with pain running down my shins.

Walking was a mighty challenge, and it wasn't just about walking; it was more complex than placing one foot in front of the other. I had to help my body and mind be in sync. I'd visually focus on where I wanted to walk and not move my head too much; otherwise, I lost that focus. I had to balance one foot as it came down and the other as it went up while keeping upright and not leaning forward. I had to balance my brain (like an air bubble in a spirit level) and keep my body moving to make the next step and navigate the terrain I was walking.

I was mindful of what was happening around me, such as passing people, cars, and other noises. My legs needed to move and bend at the knee while my arms moved in sync with them. I had to manually move the affected left leg but keep balance when it kicked wide. I'd try not to move my head or eyes, as they had to stay balanced. I felt all sensations involved within each step taken. Small objects under my foot were exaggerated - a single hair strand would feel like a piece of string that somehow found a way to tangle my foot and put me off my stride and balance. You would never usually notice this action, but I'd become super sensitive and notice everything. The sensation goes through your hip, as you acknowledge the socket movement in your pelvis.

There is so much that needs to be absorbed before you can complete that step. So, when people take it upon themselves to stop and stare to try and work out what's wrong, they are actually putting that individual off their aim/work. Every movement taken is very robotic. It does indeed all get better over time. We are not talking about days, weeks, or even months; we're talking about years.

Others informed me that I walked off my hips in my attempts at walking. I wondered what they were going on about as I walked with a wide gait. Don't get me wrong, in my early stages, this was quite correct. As the years went on and on, I noticed whilst on my treadmill one day how I didn't walk with one foot in front of the other; I was walking parallel with my hips if that makes sense. I wasn't attempting the exaggerated catwalk trot; I was rigid in my steps. It was from this moment that I realised what others meant. I acted on the action and practised walking on my treadmill while holding the sidebars with a narrower gait. It hurt my hips to perform this movement, though I knew this was the correct way to walk, and my hips would have to become accustomed to this narrower gait. Whichever of my legs was grounded in the walking movement had to be solid to the ground as it would become the balancing rod for the walking motion. I had to learn to hinge myself forward enough from my hip to make a larger forward step supported by the grounded leg. This replaced the mouse steps I had performed for the past three and a half years. I knew it wouldn't be an overnight fix; I had learnt that all recovery aspects took time. All I could do was be repetitive with the new acknowledged walk wherever I went.

Some days, I simply didn't want to step off my bed as then the struggle began. My right leg had been particularly bad, though it showed no symptoms to indicate what it could be. As soon as it was weight-bearing, I was in pain. I started doing calf muscle stretching in the hope it may loosen it and help relieve the pain. I had tried this in the past before my bleed, as I remember always having tight calves; I can't remember it helping much, though maybe I wasn't strict enough in doing them. My legs, from the knees down, have been a continuous issue for me from day one. I have experienced super-hot legs, 'Meccano' feeling legs, sore knees, balancing pin head knees, juddering knees, a lack of support from my knees, extreme pain behind my knee on the back of the right leg (feels like pulled tight ligaments), painful calf muscles - like the sensations you get after having cramp in your calf. (I can't actually remember having cramps; I just experienced the after-cramp sensation).

The rigid contender

When I first started taking a few steps, I was extremely rigid. I basically didn't bend from the waist down. I had to focus on where I was going, calculate all possibilities of distraction, stare it out and then attempt it. I carried the biggest unnatural stare - if I wanted attention this was a good method to receive it. This went on for a good three plus years. During the whole time, I was unable to move my head while walking. If I attempted this, I was thrown instantly off balance. If I wished to turn my head, I had to stop, think about the turn, do the turn, and stare to refocus, by which time the moment would have passed.

If you had seen me being assisted with my walking in my first few years, you would have noticed how I was dead straight. I would be so in the zone, so to speak, that I may not even notice you. I would also probably not be able to recognise you with my poor vision. Not by choice, I had my out-of-focus lenses on full-time.

When I refer to my walking, I'm referring to assisted walking, as I was by no means walking about independently. It took me around three years to get closer to natural looking as I walked. Due to the poor balance involved, standing was a balancing act. I would walk as if my legs were wooden sticks. I was extremely stiff, scared to move another aspect of my body as it would throw the balance out. I still could not walk and look around. I would have to stop to move my head physically.

One day, I acknowledged that I leant slightly forward with my walk, mainly due to the brain pulling me forward. I would suddenly find myself walking a bit quicker due to the forward pull by my brain. I would describe this occurrence as due to the brain knowing I was moving forward; if I were to stop suddenly, the brain would still be in motion to move forward. It seemed there was an imbalance somewhere taking place. Walking was more of a struggle when your legs continuously tried to stop you from falling. You don't want to live like this and pine for the day it will pass. It's hard work and unnatural, and the pain and sheer frustration make you want to cry.

I have injured myself many times, but I hardly ever recognise the hurt. I might have quite possibly pulled a muscle, but I would see it as a blessing that the brain did not acknowledge the injury, so I was not put back in going forward. As Thomas Wayne says to his son Bruce Wayne in Batman Begins *"Why do we fall? So, we can learn to pick ourselves up."*

I taught myself to stand tall while walking as I wanted to move away from the forward lean. Walking linked-armed was my favourite support action, knowing I had a stable, strong body supporting me. This also enabled me to add a little bit of free independent walking here and there where the circumstances were correct for me to help build my confidence in my independence.

My brain couldn't multitask because it involved moving my arms with my legs. My brain could only produce one of the actions, so my legs always won. This is where my rigid walking came from. It took around two and half years for my arms and legs to coordinate whilst walking. And even then, you could tell it was me moving the arms as the action never came from my trunk; it came from my elbows; it still wasn't very natural, though it looked better than being dead rigid. Someone had to continually remind me to move my arms, as I easily forgot, and I would return to looking rigid and stiff. Due to the slow recovery speed with my balance, it took years before my gait improved to a narrower approach; even four years post-bleed, my gait still had a wide approach. I seemed to walk from my hips, so my gait naturally followed the hip width.

Walking was very mechanical, and it hurt from the knees down. It was quite intense for a good few years. I would refer to myself as having Meccano legs as they felt so unnatural. The joints felt as though they were screwed together, and my movement was hinged.

In 2020, I started to see an improvement in my assisted walking. It was becoming more natural-looking and feeling more natural. Pain and discomfort had absorbed to only behind the knees.

With no flexibility in my legs for the first two years, even kneeling hurt. I started stretching them quite a bit as, in my way of thinking, my legs were continuously under strain from keeping me standing. I could fall at any time or trip and cause myself great damage, which I could do without. I started this around June 2019, as up until this point, I was still very unstable in attempting any stretches. All the muscles were so tight and felt shortened in length.

Some days would place me in a super low mood, usually when my right leg was playing up. It would be so painful, and no professional/specialist would know what to do. There was no visible sign of help, and this would, therefore, leave everyone confused. All I could do was rest it and continue using it as I would or even try to overuse it to make it beyond tired. My explanation for the situation was that I had a new way of using the leg; my walking was different, so the muscles had redesigned themselves. Due to taking a new walking approach after thirty-six years of walking a particular way, my calf muscles were redesigning themselves to support the body in a new way, along with the overcompensating strain for the left leg not being recognised by the brain. This was ongoing after three years; I had no indication when this would ease up. This new way took place in the first year and a half. After this time, the brain recognised the left leg, and feeling and sensation in the leg were reintroduced. The right leg had to redesign itself again, as less compensation was required. There were days to which I never wanted to stand up, not even interested in getting out of bed, as I knew the discomfort it would endure. I walked very stiff and rigid for probably the first three years, and then it started to ease. I was also starting to get worn down by it. This was still ongoing three years post-bleed to look more normal. It had no effect, no matter what I threw at it to help. I had theories on why it was causing the sensation of discomfort with added pain, mainly suggested around the muscle redesigning itself. Of course, they were only my ideas on the situation and how I would describe it. When I offered my theories to the physiotherapists, they agreed that my ideas seemed reasonable.

Even after two and a half years, the calf pain was accompanied by painful shins. My lower legs had a hot sensation; even to the touch, they were super warm.

It was the use of my legs that hindered my daily performance. From day one, they felt no longer connected to my body. My waist would sway uncontrollably if I were to put a wiggle into it, and I had to talk to myself about how to lift and move my legs. After nearly three years of practising this protocol, my waist became stronger, and its looseness faded. My legs also strengthened in how I talked them through their actions less. They became less tired so abundantly and became better at holding my weight. They still were not one hundred per cent, but a lot of light showed that I was much closer to the finish line.

At the twenty-month mark, I started concentrating more on lifting my left knee/leg when walking. My brain forgot to focus on the left leg movement when tiredness started. It was usually from this point that I scuffed my foot when walking.

Three and a half years after the bleed, I noticed the easing of the sharp ridge on the outer edge of my left foot. It would often appear as a ball on the outside of my left foot, rolling and spinning me in that particular direction.

Sometimes, you physically can't go on, but push yourself very hard to achieve it. I don't know if this was good, but I consistently did it. Occasionally, I thought, 'No, I'm not doing it,' but I mostly got on with it. Sometimes, I would cry inside as trying to walk independently was so hard. While doing this, I would try not to notice my body swaying back and forth. Most importantly, I tried to balance the entire time even though everything seemed flat (2D vision) to me. So, it was all very challenging.

Diary Entry: April 2019 - *Walking the handful of steps from my bedroom to the bathroom, took me two years to become less reliant on holding onto the walls for balance.*

It also took around two years for me to step off my bed without being pulled backwards back onto the bed. I also had quite bad calf cramp sensations, which started to ease around this time. I used to leave my bed by using a four-wheel walker. I then stopped using this and managed a couple of steps to grab my sideboard and then the wall through to the bathroom; I started trying to do this task without any help and support, which did come together with time.

I used my treadmill daily. I purchased it about seven months after coming home to help recover. It took around eighteen months before I started to improve on this device. I'd hold onto the bars on either side for my balance, and over the years, I'd attempt using just one hand for balance, alternating which arm I would use to hold on. After three and a half years, I could use it for a handful of steps without my hands on a very slow speed. It took a long time, using a lot of determination and enthusiasm, to achieve this goal. However, I never gave up on trying. My left leg was sluggish, and I had to train it to step higher and be more straight away from stepping wide.

After two years of using the treadmill, my sway became less. However, it was still there when trying to walk, and this seemed to hinder me from walking independently.

My left leg felt seventy per cent corrected around the three-year mark. The ground recognised my foot more, and the outwards flick when walking, which the leg liked to practice, was becoming less. My left leg determined my walk pattern. It was the leader. After three years, little improvement occurred, though the left leg felt stronger. I became extremely tired when walking, which always made my left leg less functional. My body weight would still pull me forward even when I had stopped walking. So, I would stop and wobble forward as, for some reason, my body felt as though it still wanted to move in that direction. If I wanted to bend forward, I would probably want to go over, as something was pulling my head to the ground. I pushed my walking ability with exercises to encourage strengthening of the left leg and both in the muscles and signals to the brain. I always encountered a rigid sensation in my left calf, which eased quite a bit after three years.

You must live every day like everything is fine when you really want to cry most of the time. No one else would understand this, so it was super frustrating contending with it and not being able to share the struggle without sounding weak or pathetic.

Diary Entry: March 2020

Even after nearly three years, my legs physically hurt, and they genuinely didn't want to be used. There were days I never really wanted to get out of bed due to their discomfort. I would constantly feel light on my feet. I never understood how I could be so light and vulnerable to any unknown/planned movement, being my weight. The human body carries weight, whatever your weight, so being breezy outside should not be enough to send you over. In my case, it was. Throughout my recovery, my legs felt as light as feathers and were very springy in sensation.

Diary Entry: October 2020

Morning weighing - I weighed myself most days upon waking after the first year of being home from the hospital. I needed assistance initially to get onto the scales as I would shake too much. It was within my third year that I was able to step onto the scales with ease. It took less effort and was more natural. I was not completely satisfied with the movement of stepping on and off the scales, though it was promising that I would be close to the finish line.

Diary Entry: December 2020

Walking behind someone proves very difficult when the individual continually stops to look behind to check you're okay. My brain is still in moving forward motion to then suddenly stop, throwing it out of action with its thoughts. My example with this situation would be following my Mum around the supermarket and she has one of those pull-along baskets. Every time she slowed down, I felt like I was catapulting forward but yet slowing down myself. My brain was always counterbalancing the action. I kept telling myself that over time, the brain sensation would slowly understand the action, and I would feel the sensation less.

It was super hard to have anyone understand the real struggles with walking. When humans cancel out their surroundings to concentrate on the desired action, we subconsciously know our surroundings and who's in the picture. When I take this action, I really do cancel out my surroundings. If I subconsciously knew what was going on, it would be enough to send me off balance, which causes me to stagger and usually causes injury to my right calf leg.

I had sore heels from the hospital. As time passed, it occurred to me that maybe my sore heels resulted from my legs being a dead weight when I lay on my back for long periods. My lower legs would be very warm and slightly throbbing. Though I could move my legs and control them, I did not have any temperature control over them.

2021 saw me taking steadier walking steps without being link-armed with someone. My independence was slowly emerging. I still required the support of someone by my side, as I was still thrown off my walking rhythm with slight disturbances on my walking path regarding terrain. However, I was making more solo attempts; these were only a few steps. Still, I would consider the improved scenario stage one to reach my independent walking. I knew I had a fair bit to go, though it was a massive achievement to be at the stage which I was.

Four years post-bleed notes - Right lower leg

The calf is slightly swollen and sore from the inner calf behind the knee area, around to the front of the knee. The shin throbs and is very achy throughout and tingly at times. I have had the area looked at by physiotherapists, who couldn't find anything wrong. An ultrasound scan showed nothing was wrong. Paracetamol and ibuprofen don't help. Stretching helps with relief for that moment. I experience early morning cramping.

I had experienced many different sensations where my legs were concerned, and during my fourth year, it was an intense fatigued sensation. The brain would switch off from helping my legs perform the walking action, and they were like spaghetti from the hips, which made life that much harder. Most days, they were super tired and felt a heavy weight which ran along their shins. It was hard getting them to lift to perform any walking actions. Concentrating on helping my legs would use up all my energy, resulting in me having to lay down. The brain would often feel numb when working, and it would have no more strength to continue with new actions - even if the action was as little as getting a glass of water.

My right leg caused more grievances. I pin-pointed the pain to the shin, which has now moved into the knee. Once before, during the year 2021, around November, the pain moved into the knee joint. With the pain moving about, I hold onto the thought of it improving.

My cerebellum very much dictated to my left leg. I didn't have full control over its movements. This was extremely hard to explain to others as I seemed awkward or making excuses. My legs would shake quite vigorously upon standing from seated. It took three years to calm down, though it was still not entirely gone. I noticed it was mainly the left leg, which felt more like a judder from the knee down now, which would cause uncomfortable feelings. I would look at this, and instead of feeling down that it was still causing discomfort, it was improving, and hopefully, by this time next year, it would have nearly gone.

By January 2022, I was still particularly struggling with my walking. I'm not one hundred per cent certain to what the actual cause was for this occurrence, though my left leg had become extremely heavy and dictating to my movements. It's like all my leg bones are lead rods. The leg is particularly heavy and even though I think it's walking, it's actually not and I will catch it on stepping, making me stagger. It's almost like the brain is working faster than the actual steps taken.

My legs had become particularly bad in cold weather. It was almost like my temperature gauge was damaged. If I got slightly cold, my legs went extremely cold, and I would be shivering so much that I would struggle to make any walking movements. My feet would feel like blocks of ice, and I would continuously shiver.

I can't stress enough how much my legs hurt. Even at nearly seven years post-bleed, I struggled with over-exhausted legs. Upon waking, my shins would be super achy, like I had been walking all night. It was hard to accept that my legs were such a problem, along with my right leg calf pain, which was still present all day long. We all use our legs like second nature, but I couldn't. Just walking from my bedroom to the kitchen would cause them super discomfort.

Sometimes, others may see me walking with assistance, but this would have only involved a short distance. Like anything you do in life, you have good days and bad. Some days, I saw myself walking well and managing a short distance over my usual handful of steps. Still, this taste of life would reward me with multiple bad days straight after. I may manage to walk a little further on a good day, but I'm not walking easily; I'm still majorly struggling, and any onlooker will notice that I struggle with my walking. You will not have noted all my stops, sit-down breaks I've taken when possible, or wobbly episodes. Even when I link arms with somebody, it's sometimes a challenge to walk a handful of steps. Any unexpected movement my company incurs has a knock-on effect on me. I wobble and pull. My Dad was my main help with walking, and it's no secret that I damaged his hip from the constant pulling. It would make me sad that I struggle with the simplest of tasks.

"It's up to me to manage my expectations and it's up to my brain to manage repairs."

Jo Ulczak

Chapter Six | Acknowledgement

Reading my own notes was quite motivational. It revealed how far I had come in my recovery, made me smile, and reminded me of everything I had achieved.

You must acknowledge everything you do and talk to the brain through situations to show it that an improvement has occurred. All small steps lead to great achievements.

An example of acknowledging improvement was my gym attempts. It took me around six months of going to the gym before my muscles started realising I was using them. Sometimes, you must believe in the improvements to stay positive. You don't see them every day and can go for weeks and not see or feel any improvement, and then, out of the blue, it appears. You may notice your stance is slightly more robust, or the four steps you take across the kitchen are that much better. The improvement often proved minor, an action we may not even consider. However, when taken away and you regain this, you definitely see its importance. It's a piece of the jigsaw on the path towards recovery.

If anything, I was learning more and more about the human body - the connections between all the muscles, tendons, ligaments, etc., involved in our movements. This could be something as simple as picking up a pen. The amount of multitasking the brain does goes unnoticed in our everyday lives. It's only now that I'm acknowledging this due to having to rebuild the body, and multitasking is not the brain's favourite pastime.

I had to retrain all sensations towards my left side of my body. My brain had to acknowledge and understand all sensations incorporated by this side.

I was wheeled into the garden in 2017 during the summer. In 2018, I used a Zimmer frame and then a four-wheeled walker, and in 2019, I used the support of one of my parents. I was improving, but it was super slow. In 2019, I wasn't manoeuvring as I imagined, but I was manoeuvring more and more independently. It was slow and extremely frustrating, but it was improving. You just had to recognise this and acknowledge it.

I don't think outsiders fully appreciated the struggles which I would undergo daily. Moving an object from the worktop to the table or room to room was nearly impossible. I did not have the stability or vision to carry out such simple tasks. I looked fine so therefore I must be fine. If that were the case, I would not have written my book. I was so unstable it was hard to stay positive, and I had to plan my daily movements.

If I had plans to be out for some of a day, I would have to be aware of the toilet location and business of the establishment, that it was relatively flat-surfaced, that it was wide enough for me to walk link-armed and that the lighting was going to be sufficient for me to see. I had to choreograph my movements, which took a lot of energy. Anxiety, if not controlled, would play a vital part in wearing me down before any movements had even taken place. As hard as this was, I would still do it. I wanted as much of a normal life as possible, and if my family and friends were willing to help me, I would try my hardest.

There were times when I just couldn't push forward; after all, I was no superhero, so I would be a fool to think I would be able to achieve everything I would have wanted to. The first two and half years of my bleed were the hardest. Improvement definitely has to be acknowledged to keep you on the path to recovery. For me, this could be while out in a store. My vision would hold out for longer, walking about outside (assisted), my legs would not hurt as much, my headache around my eyes had eased away, etc. All of these took a minimum of a couple of years to achieve. I would have appreciated it if my independent walking ability or my vision had been corrected after this time. Still, in my situation, it wasn't the case. Improvement was noted in month blocks, so I may not really see the improvement every week. It would be more like six months. Then, it may only be something minor, like the steps taken across the room being taken stronger. Such a small acknowledgement of improvement was more than enough to show me that I was moving in the right direction to recovery.

Staying strong is the hardest task in the recovery process. The only way to move forward is to actually move forward. It is so easy to sit back and do nothing to help yourself - I was never wired up this way. I wanted to do stuff to aid my recovery, which may just be going to the supermarket. However, this would take an immense amount of energy, and for me, it was a task I would do before the bleed; therefore, I wanted to stay with the programme. Social interaction and involvement were all part of my recovery - it was cognitive therapy. Just the store lighting was part of my healing process as I struggled with store lighting. In my sixth year of recovery, I purchased some prescription glasses with a blue tint, which helped with artificial lighting. When my vision started holding out for longer, I would then know I had passed the next hurdle. It took time, as everything does. There were so many times that I would think that I did not want to go to the store today (like many outings), but I would find the motivation to do so. I was no hero, I was just trying to get better.

Note to oneself - November 18th, 2019

My walking improvement is noticed today by my stronger posture while walking and standing. Every day moving forward in recovery was hard. You want to be living your days as you once did. The brain is in denial that this is not currently possible, but instead, 'I can achieve anything' was the chain of thought I took. It took a good two/three years before I started realising and acknowledging that I may not be able to reach my desired destination in the same manner as I would have once upon a time. But it did not ever register that I would not get to my destination, just that I would have to take a different route. I would have to hold onto these positive thoughts as it was these which kept me sane.

Diary Entry: January 2020

When out and about, shop lighting still affects me quite badly, and I become extremely tired.

The main person who can help you get better is yourself. It doesn't matter at times how much input comes from others; it's how you approach the situation. I tried to live every day to the best of my capability. Improvement happened for me only after months and months of input. If I didn't acknowledge these improvements, no matter how small a scale they were on, I would continually feel there was no improvement. I had to tell myself consistently and others of my improvements; I had to talk it out, I think, to make it real to the brain. Even though it was real, I had to inform myself physically. I had to push myself to take part in daily living as I felt this was what was making me stronger.

Writing bullet points and short paragraphs on my recovery throughout was my outlet and therapy for improvement. It's what helped me get through my ordeal. It was my way of acknowledging the improvements.

I never used to cry out for the old me or even ask, "Why me?" I just got on with it all. Yes, it was a very unfortunate occurrence. Not everyone encounters an AVM within the brain, and not everyone is fortunate enough to tell the journey they undertook. So, being fortunate to have my parents' strong support, I promised to share this encounter in the hope that it would offer determination and motivation to others in whatever form they require.

Acknowledgement log - January 2020

I began to acknowledge my improvement in balance and how I was becoming stronger. My treadmill walking is becoming more consistent unassisted. I have noticed that the right calf muscle may be under stress from leaning off the right hip when walking unaided. It's weight-bearing and takes a lot of strain to compensate for me not falling.

My stair-walking is improving. I am not swaying as much in the back of my skull, which has decreased in intensity. This is what used to encourage me to overlean. At times, it appears still, allowing me to achieve my task. My supermarket walking is much better as I'm not finding the need to hold on to things as often or having the need to require a trolley continually for balance.

Improvement is not about taking more steps at a time; it's more about doing the steps taken that much better. Over time, the steps and stance became stronger. I was noticing every stone under my foot less and less. I no longer identified every section of the terrain I walked as dangerous.

Diary Entry: - August 2020

Acknowledging my left leg seemed to be the answer to my right calf muscle pain decreasing. When I placed all my thoughts onto the left leg, my right leg pain would ease. I started thinking that I was obsessed with my right calf and was subconsciously creating pain and discomfort. I was over weight-bearing on this leg and had to balance out my pelvis to achieve an equal weight shift among my legs. It was from doing this that I would notice a difference in the pain. I had practised stretching every day from January 2018 until now, and I still wasn't mega flexible; my chain of thought was, to discourage accidents from occurring to my legs as I was of poor mobility, it made perfect sense to have flexibility in my legs to help avoid this occurring. No physio could see anything incorrect with the leg, nor could my doctor. I also had a scan on it, which, of course, showed nothing. My last resort was massage, as I felt it may release something. I can't say it did anything.

I quite often acknowledged all the injuries I could have encountered during my recovery. I would have visions of the worst possible scenarios, though I never allowed the visions to distract me from trying. After all, they were only visions.

When pulled backwards, I take a step backwards rather than just fall in motion. I never used to take the steps to stabilise myself, I would just fall. I can stand comfortably at the sink to wash and clean my teeth. I used to have to hold onto the sink to keep me steady. When placing toothpaste onto my toothbrush, I would have to lean onto the sink as I never had the balance just to stand. After three years, I started to practice standing with my one leg whilst cleaning my teeth. I was, of course, no good at this, though it was a huge improvement when looking back over the years. It was also an improvement in my multitasking ability.

I've acknowledged that if doing nothing is going to help my recovery, then resting and doing nothing is what I will do.

I had symptoms which left me unable to do things. This could be because I couldn't use my left arm or leg to complete the task. These movements came into play over time - that's months or years- and I could do what was required again. By no means was I doing it identically to before my bleed, though I was doing it in its new fashion. Just being able to do something again is a massive achievement. I felt such satisfaction after being unable to carry out the action for so long.

Improvement was recognised when standing to talk to someone. My gait became narrower instead of wide as I tried to balance.

Every time I notice an improvement, albeit in baby steps, I question how excited I am about this improvement. Was I as excited about my last improvement? I couldn't often understand how this improvement was bigger than my last. Improvement is not how we imagine an improvement. While I hope to improve my walking independently, my balance and even my vision, I will receive an improvement that may not look as I envisioned- such as my new taste buds. I can now taste that my tea has sugar. It may not be an improvement I'm longing for, but I'm sure if it never happened, I would adapt. Even so, it's an improvement that proves I am repairing my body.

I had to hold onto these minor improvements and inform myself that it all led to the bigger picture, like the jigsaw, which seemed to be refitting back together.

Diary Entry: February 2021

The last day of January 2021 was a miserable rainy day. I went into the local store with my Mum and it was the first time since the bleed I could acknowledge a form of stability in my brain. I walked a few steps, but there was no sideways sway. It was almost like the magnet was stuck in neutral within my brain, not allowing me to sway. It felt normal again regarding not being pulled to the side. I smiled. Sadly, it only lasted for this moment.

As I step up onto my step block, I don't get pulled backwards as much when stepping back down. If anything, my odds of not receiving the pulled-back sensation are higher than my odds of receiving it.

Diary Entry: March 2021

Reading through past notes, I have documented - I see how I sway through my left side internally on numerous occasions. It's March 2021, and I no longer recognise this sensation on my left side. This encourages me and provides positive evidence. I acknowledged this improvement and documented it in my brain. Although, it's only a slight improvement from a situation that was quite a prominent symptom; not recognising this symptom shows me it has eased away in a manner I hadn't acknowledged.

Acknowledging my symptoms improving didn't just relate to all the positive improvements; it also related to symptoms that didn't improve and implementing ideas on how to work with the new normal for the injured party.

One symptom which I continually struggled with was my left eye. Now, how do I make life easier for myself with a symptom which has such a great impact on the body? My sight was distorted when working with my right eye, and my eyes didn't align. Seeing through it caused pain in the back of my brain. I found that patching it off really helped the situation, though it had its consequences. As I have mentioned previously, covering my left lens over my glasses solved the problem of my distorted and double vision, as my right eye had no concerns, so I could see pretty well. The downside was that due to the shut off left eye, I'd lose the signal on the left side for my body to function when walking. This made walking around whilst patching the left eye off rather difficult. It would see me spin to the left as I struggled to have any sensation in my left, and it would see me bash into most things on my left as I didn't recognise I had a left side. When stationed, patching the left eye was fantastic and particularly great for reading. I acknowledged how beneficial it was to patch the left eye. Also, I acknowledged how it wasn't beneficial for physically moving around. I had to accept this acknowledgement as hard as it was to and realise there was no answer to this situation. I had other symptoms, which I would also acknowledge as not completely improving, one being my left arm. It would just randomly twitch, stemming from the shoulder socket. I had no idea as to when it was going to happen and sometimes, I could go weeks without noticing it, though now and again I would have episodes of this uncontrollable twitch. At nearly seven years post-bleed, I acknowledged it might be a lifelong symptom. Also, when the body was over-tired, it would appear.

"Progress is progress no matter how small."

Henry Ford

Chapter Seven | Not an Overnight Fixture

Many individuals experience life-changing circumstances affecting their bodies. I'm not special as in being one of them.

I'm the act everyone is waiting to see. If only I charged. Everything I do is done awkwardly; I'm the individual who can join you for dinner, though the way I make an entrance and sit at the table is undoubtedly awkward.

Staring was a good trait, and I did a lot of it, mainly because I needed to carefully process the information I received due to my damaged vision, which onlookers could refer to as staring as they watched my every move. I was also one for facial expressions when concentrating. Most of the time, I wasn't even aware of pulling these interesting expressions. I started to ease them off after a couple of years; others mainly noticed them with my attempted walking. It took two years to regain my features, and my natural expression reappeared. I was lucky enough to have individuals sometimes stop and stare at me. I wasn't the most graceful assisted walker, so I can imagine there would be a few curious minds out there, especially when I did my cha-cha-cha past them. I labelled myself the performing monkey as I felt like I was on constant watch by others, and linking arms with my company for support made me feel like I was swinging from a branch.

What had happened to me was quite a serious, traumatic, and severe occurrence, placing me in a very challenging position. Only my light-hearted banter towards my situation kept my spirits high and the people around me in an okay place of mind. No one wants to be accompanied by a low-mood individual daily. Unless you have laughs along the way, there's just no point.

I lost all body strength and independence, and I wasn't even forty years old. It felt like I had lost my take on life as I could no longer pursue it in the manner I had mapped out. After three years of toying with the idea of independence, I started to get emotional with the slow speed of the recovery, though I still couldn't cry. I was continually moving in the right direction; each step was just small. Others say *"it doesn't matter how big the steps are as long as they are in the right direction"* as said in marvels S.H.I.E.L.D. but can you imagine how hard and soul destroying it is for that individual? It felt as though I had been crying internally for three years, but I masked it away.

I defied all odds by surviving the bleed, and I'm convinced I can defy all odds by reaching a life of independence. No one said the path would be easy, and it's by far anything but easy. I have encountered many situations where you feel the statement of 'pick on the weak' is very appropriate.

The general rule that the medics continually informed me of was that two years usually shows most of the improvement. For me, this wasn't the case. I was defying all odds with recovery. No one could advise on my recovery as no one actually knew. I was advised of time frames and would disregard them because although I could not achieve something in a suggested time frame, it did not mean I would never achieve it. I was past the suggested repair stages and still showed positive results. How the bleed injured me enabled me to understand the body; I had a connection to all parts of my body, and I could feel them. I believed that it was possible to overcome this major hindrance to my life. Yes, I accepted after several years that I would never have the same limitations and abilities as before my bleed, though that was never going to stop me from trying.

I believe my recovery stepped up a mark during my third-year post-bleed. I had to keep enthusiasm, motivation, and determination as my top priorities throughout my entire recovery period, and not for one second did I ever lose hope in my goal of achieving a form of independence. If I had believed in the two-year suggestion, I would have easily lost hope and determination in my recovery after passing this point.

We all heal and recover at different speeds. For example, a person who may not show much improvement within the first six months after a bleed may show much improvement within six to twelve months after the bleed.

In my immediate days of consciousness, I continually stated that the brain was so intelligent that it would rebuild; there was no way I could not create a new me. I had no medical background, I did not actually know anything, though I had this intense sensation/feeling that I was going to be okay. What had happened to me gave me an intelligence on my body. I believed that I would fix it and that it was impossible not to fix it. I don't know if this belief helped me through the coming years, but I believed so much in the human body's intelligence that it kept me strong in the darkest hours.

Whoever told me that recovery was going to be slow were not wrong. Everyone in the care/specialist departments would advise on this. In my early days of coming home from the hospital, I used to believe that if my eyes could be corrected, it would then have a knock-on effect on my balance and walking. Repair never happened in this manner. It was like the damaged area of brain was a sponge and absorbed all the symptoms at the same speed, which was on the slow meter. I never lost the ability to walk, only I could now only achieve it with assistance. I wanted to walk independently again and I never stopped believing that this would happen for me.

My struggle never went away, I would still be struggling just as hard, though in some light it was a lesser struggle. I remember the sensation in January 2021, how my whole left side of the brain felt as though it had dropped. My bleed occurred in the back bottom left of my brain, my cerebellum, though at times, it felt as if the entire left side of my brain was affected. I put it down to my vision, which had to feed through to the back of the brain, making the left side extremely tired as it was injured compared to the right.

We are all guilty of taking life for granted; just those first few steps you take every time from leaving your home to go out are unthought steps. We do not need to think it out, we just get on with it naturally. Only when something happens that strips you back to basics do you realise how clever we really are. Seeing how slow brain recovery is only makes me believe we are always regenerating, building new pathways. We always say that we are continually learning throughout life, though we don't put much thought into the process. It's just a passing comment. Being in my situation of recovering from a brain haemorrhage, stripped me back beyond basics. I have always felt for me that pathways had to be rebuilt and then filled. It's through this slow achievement that you see how clever the brain is. After pathways are destroyed, how could you imagine them reforming? I couldn't stand without swaying or shaking, I couldn't take three steps without swaying over. Though I did progress past this episode within recovery. This is evidence that we heal and that the brain works a new pattern regarding pathways.

Excuses

I would be seen as making an excuse if I could not achieve something; however, it meant I genuinely could not do it. My frequent complaints were that my legs were particularly sore and hurt, my knees were painful, my left leg had a habit of flicking out to the left while stepping occasionally, I'd be extremely fatigued, my muscles all hurt, and my brain could not comprehend any more instructions. If it were as simple as sending confident commands to the brain, I would be much further in my recovery. Unfortunately, it's not that easy... 'Don't run before you can walk' is appropriate for this scenario.

The brain is super unpredictable about what action it will take. Just because I know I want to walk down the drive and I know how to achieve this does not mean I will achieve it. If my brain is distracted in any manner, it will take me off my path of action.

Struggle had always been my shadow since day one when my brain bled. Every action I took during my day was extremely tiring. No, it was not me being lazy; I don't think not going to the bathroom when you're bursting is lazy. It was so challenging. In my earlier days, I would need someone to supervise and assist me everywhere; as time went on, the constant assistance lessened to what it was. I was too unstable and unpredictable with my movements to venture alone far. It was hard for me to venture anywhere during the day, so if I needed the bathroom, I was... well, I couldn't go. I had to time and calculate every movement to ensure all bases were covered and safe to pursue. We never think about these little gestures beforehand; we just deal with them when they happen.

So, knowing a friend has taken me out for coffee, what do I do during the outing if I need a wee? I can't just get up and go like I used to. If I'm with male company, they can assist me to the toilet, but then I'm alone. I question myself, "Do I really want them to assist me? And can I manage the alone part due to my balance?" Well, if I'm bursting, what choice do I have? When with female company, it's much easier. And then there's the stairs challenge. What if the toilets are up a flight of stairs? The list goes on with possible scenarios. The solution in extreme situations is to use the downstairs disabled toilet (if there is one on offer). However, you usually have to ask a staff member for the key, which again adds time to going to the toilet. You no doubt have to go to the counter to ask for this but remember, I can't walk without assistance; it just adds to the toilet challenge. I once waited to use an accessible toilet due to the ladies toilets being upstairs, with a mini walk down a corridor to the actual toilets. I couldn't walk unaided, so it was far too much for me to take on, along with being a shaky mess and not having full vision. A lady also walked up to use the disabled toilet but looked capable of using the upstairs toilets. She trotted over, unlike me, who was assisted over and held by my friend to keep me stable. She had the cheek to inform me that there were upstairs toilets to use whilst getting out her key for the disabled restroom. I thought to myself, 'Is this lady serious?' Unlike my unstable self, she looked more than capable of using the upstairs restroom. She could have had underlying symptoms which prevented her from going upstairs; it could be the case of 'don't judge a book by its cover', or it could be exactly as it seemed.

I would have to contend with this behaviour from others every time I left the house. I saw individuals seemingly take advantage of benefits granted to the unfortunate, which were generally relied on and appreciated. I was now one of these individuals and received this poor treatment of others firsthand on many occasions. To be questioned when it's clear as day as to what the concern is for me by an individual who was a potential fraud was pretty insulting.

I put on two stone from leaving the hospital, but my weight was the least of my concerns. Looking at me, you probably wouldn't even notice too much that I was this much heavier. In the first year, I didn't do much about it; in the second year, I tried different eating regimes, though it would all stem back to the fact that I wasn't very mobile and, therefore, couldn't really exercise. I lost half a stone in the second year. The year offered very little reward for my weight situation, given the food sacrifice. It made it evident that it had to do with exercise. I did what I could in this department as I was usually quite active, so I never found it too much of a problem finding enthusiasm for it. I could have been much larger and heavier as I went from active to non-active overnight, but I was content with myself and knew I could address this in the long run when the time was right. I knew that I would return to the activity world when my independence was available.

Being at home with my parents with no ties made it easier for my recovery, as I had no overheads, be it financially or via a relationship, etc. At the time, it was hard to see my situation from this angle. It was only as time went on that I saw the bigger picture. I was exactly where I needed to be to overcome this mishap.

Each of my parents played an important role in helping me, and I received massive support from them. They kept me involved with society no matter how hard I felt it was towards the occasions; I feel I would not have improved to the extent I have if I cowered away every time. However, try standing whilst the back of your brain is juddering, your legs from the knee down are shaking but also really ache, and your right calf muscle feels like exploding out of your leg. And there is a person who is supporting you with a linked arm as you can't actually see fully as your vision is damaged. It's an example that I doubt anyone can associate with, as it's not something you can go and do to put yourself in my shoes.

It was always bizarre to be a passenger in a car. I had to accept that this would be the new normal for me for a while. I always did my share of driving before my brain bleed. I enjoyed being the driver and taking my family and friends about their day. Being a passenger always made me feel slightly lazy, but I had no choice but to play that part. When you have driven your entire life, it's quite life-changing when it's taken away from you.

I would calculate all my movements, obstacles in my way, distance, and pavements involved. I perceived puddles as lakes, stones as boulders, and tiny streams as rivers. Oh, how I would make others laugh with my exaggerated descriptions.

Unless I was detoured around obstacles in my pathway, I would just walk into them. I'd see the obstacle, maybe a puddle or stone pillar, which would require me to detour around, but the processing process would result in me walking into the situation that I was trying to avoid. There seemed to be a problem with processing information and recalculating a new route. It came down to the brain still being unable to multitask.

The number of times I had soggy feet and mild bruises on my left side where I had just walked into something or through a puddle. It was ever disheartening, though I would think no one saw, so what does it matter?

I had a shower seat because the base of the shower was too slippery to stand on, and I also had a handrail installed to help me stand. I still use these items. I'm ageing, after all.

I had very poor signals from my lower legs to my brain. I would imagine I could walk on hot coal or barefoot in the snow (not that I actually did either of these) and not feel anything. There seemed to be a disruption with my pain signal concerning my lower limbs. This has improved over the years. I was three and a half years post-bleed when I realised I could feel the shower basin under my feet.

Two Year Recognitions

The body was in denial of what was going on towards it as it knows from past situations that when you are unwell, it's only a matter of days, weeks, or months before you heal up and are better. When the two-year point arrived, the brain started realising that it really was going to be a slow recovery. Nevertheless, it was going to get better. Finding enthusiasm for recovery became harder; it was still there, just harder to grab hold of. I hadn't been one for tears for over a year, but the sensation was back two years post-bleed. I just wanted to cry and make everything easier for me. If only it were that easy, and if only I could cry.

I still couldn't independently walk to our local shops, which were a ten-minute walk away. At this point in recovery, the two-year mark, the situation was starting to hit home. Keeping positive with my outlook was probably one of the best recipes for helping me reach my goal. It's super hard sometimes to keep a smile on, as each day has a feeling of deja vu.

Diary Entry: February 2019

My lower back and left side are still constantly sore after nearly two years.

I was asked by a physio a couple of years post-bleed if I could jump. Was I able to leave the ground? I had never thought of this as I had never needed to perform a jump; I struggled to walk, so I guess jumping was off my radar. Taking on board the question, I tried a jump, and to my surprise, I was unable to do this. I was shocked; my head was so weighted it didn't allow me to leave the ground, and my legs also felt like lead. I held onto the kitchen worktop and tried again. It took months and months of practice before I could manage a small jump whilst holding on. My knees didn't like to bend, so I didn't have the spring action, which would aid me in leaving the ground. I questioned how the impact of the jump action could cause injury to the body, as my body was very damaged and weak. The effect a jump has on your muscles and joints is quite strong, so I didn't over-perform this action. It was only occasionally I would practice a jump. I couldn't see myself entering any sack races soon, so I decided not to pursue this action as it hurt my knees and ankles quite a bit. This was the same for hopping, which was impossible to do with my balance and could only be performed on my right leg whilst holding on to something. My left leg didn't like leaving the ground, along with being super heavy. It took months and months to act on either of these tasks.

Diary Entry: April 2019

The 'Falling Tree' saying applies to me at times. If I wish to place a sock on my left foot, for example, I just get swept off my feet and go left.

I'm one of those individuals who revisits any mishaps. If I don't succeed the first time, I will keep trying until I do. I guess this is where repetition comes into play. I would practice many things like the balance board, which I purchased a couple of years post-bleed as advised by a physio. I would practice daily or every other day as I had so many actions to practice that I couldn't manage them all daily. Some of my actions practised took years before I started recognising improvement. I somehow found the motivation and enthusiasm to keep the practice of the actions alive. My balance board was also a step block, and when you removed the board's feet from the centre and placed them on either end, you could transform it into a step block. I used this device most days and, on some occasions, I used it more than once in a day. When the board was a step block, I'd practice standing with one foot on the floor, the other resting on the board, stepping up onto the board, and then stepping backwards back down to the floor. I would exaggerate my arm movements by using the opposite arm to the leg.

At the beginning of performing this action, I would have a chair on either side of the board as I was very good at swaying sideways. Doing this gave me a safety net, and I would have something to grab if I was to sway. After about ten months, I removed the chairs and placed my step board on the floor between my bed and the wall. I was very good at swaying right when I placed my right leg on the board.

The brain didn't like my left side, so when my left foot was on the floor, my brain freaked out as the left leg was expected to bear weight. This action would see the brain pull me backwards, and on occasion, a backwards step would turn into a rod sensation, so it would feel like I had a rod running from my brain to my heel on my left side. This sensation switched my brain off, and I would fall to the left onto my bed.

Now, if I were to weight bear on my right leg and rest my left foot on the board, my brain would still freak out as the left foot was lifted and positioned slightly forward and higher than my right foot on the floor. Whichever way I attempted, my brain would freak out, pulling me backwards and usually taking a few steps backwards. It took years of practice before it calmed down to a controllable level, though it never entirely went away. When converted into a balance board, it took me around two and a half years before stepping onto it and performing an improved balance action with assistance.

2019 was the year where I started to see minor improvements with my symptoms. I saw my inner body sway sensations reduce to only being noted on the left side of the body, especially when lying down. Fast forward the year and it had gone back to being on both sides of the body, though it had calmed.

It was only in March 2019 that my left leg started to be recognised by the brain. The balance board that I had purchased was proving to be very beneficial.

Up until March 2019, I couldn't turn my head when crossing the road to check for traffic or cyclists; I had to rely on my hearing and walking companion - this year started to see me accomplish this taken-for-granted task.

Gym notes

I joined our local gym the following year, post-bleed. I wasn't in a stable state, though I felt strengthening my body would aid me in getting to this goal. My Dad would take me as I could not go alone, and I would be helped in the gym by an instructor. My left side would judder quite badly when working; it was also hard to stand in position on machinery such as the cross trainer as I would sway left and right, and my feet wouldn't stay positioned. After a year of attending the gym, I stood steadier on a cross trainer; my left shoulder wasn't as alien to my body on arm machines, and I was seeing my way around the equipment more clearly. When I joined the gym, it had all been a blur. Though the signal processing from my eyes to my brain was super slow. This was a problem in general, though it seemed to stand out to me at the gym.

Improvement was slow and minimal, though it was an improvement. I'd practice every day, and for the first few years, my Dad would work with me every single day to supervise and help me. I was obsessed with overcoming my situation and felt the same two years later. Each day, I'd work on balance and core work and do one/two hours on it. I didn't spend the entire day, as that would make the repetitiveness of it all even more boring than it already was.

Three years later, everything started becoming that much harder. I required more rest and days where I did very little. I was becoming worn out.

My legs got particularly hot from the knees down. It was a nightmare when it was sunny - like I was on fire. My temperature signal seemed damaged.

Being told after three years that I was hardly likely to see much improvement in the future is not what an individual wishes to hear. After the hard work, determination and time given to my recovery, I was not willing to throw the towel in on it yet. If I had walked away from that meeting with that on board, I would have been in a much different place from where I am now. I took a day to absorb and digest the information and turn it all around in my mind. I wasn't accepting their prognosis as it was information from an individual who saw me once a year for maybe thirty minutes. I knew I had much more improvement to go and was far from giving up on making a life for myself. It was not only me who dedicated myself to my recovery; it was family and friends, too. If anything, it stoked the fire to continue with what I had been doing in favour of my recovery. Maybe it was a psychological mind game manoeuvre to tell me I wasn't going to get much better than I already was, in the hope I would fight on, or maybe it was simply the believed truth, as from going off past cases like me, it was usually the outcome.

I could feel this wasn't going to be the case with myself; I could genuinely feel my brain was repairing, and it just required time. It's easy to highlight all the negatives within the day. However, we hardly give ourselves credit and acknowledgement for our accomplishments. I could sit at the end of the day and go on about how hard it was, how much effort I had to place into my actions, how much it would hurt me mentally and physically, how much I was crying inside, etc. However, I never sat at the end of the day and told myself how well I walked, how natural I was standing, how much easier it was getting up off the chair, how well I walked the five steps from the front door to the outside steps, etc. How often do we sit and tell ourselves positives?

Not everyone knew I was repairing from a brain haemorrhage. After three years of struggle, it was becoming more accepted by myself.

Medics explained my situation in the early days as road works. I had to imagine I had come upon some roadworks, and I had to reroute my journey. This example has always stuck with me as it's so true. In my immediate day stages of recovery, as well as professionals informing me that it was unlikely I would repair to the stage I wished to; they also said that I may not retrieve my walking or that my eyes may not correct. All of which no one wishes to hear, and, like any human being, I would cry (if I could) at being informed of such negative news. You can question if it was negative or realistic, as it was probably more realistic. However, in my experience, I would probably stick to wording future improvements in a friendlier and considerate tone.

Within my third year of recovery, I noticed slightly greater improvements. They were still minor in the grand scheme of things, though it felt like all the repetitive exercises I had been doing were starting to take effect. My balance had improved very slightly, enabling me to perform many exercises slightly better. Improvements are acknowledged more, and it's only now that I am seeing greater improvements. For example, when taking my daily vitamins, I use my left hand to pick them up, and my right hand is used to hold and drink from my cup or water bottle. I am becoming able to pick vitamins up with my left hand, something I couldn't do in my immediate time from the bleed.

During this recovery year in 2020, the world was hit by COVID-19, a flu virus that originated in China. There was controversy on whether it was man-made or transmitted by eating a species unfamiliar to the human body (like a bat or snake). We will never know the actual truth. This whereabouts started in January 2020 placing my recovery a little on hold. Venturing to public establishments was advised to be avoided. There would be no gym or swimming available to me for a while. Instead, I created a home workout routine for myself. I looked at the situation as not being a setback to me or a hindrance to my recovery but more a rest period. Until then, I had been performing exercises nonstop to aid my recovery. I would use this situation to my advantage, rest more, and perform different exercises. I would concentrate more on my balance and walking and try to improve this for myself.

I watched YouTube and searched for seated exercises, methods which I had not been able to tackle due to my stability. I felt I had not done much work with my upper body. Pretty much everything I did was to strengthen my legs. I was taking a new approach towards gaining my independence.

As the months went on during the pandemic, I started to question if the mindset of much-needed rest was the right approach. I was continually tired and lethargic; my body didn't want to attempt much. I was starting to see that continually doing things with my day was actually quite beneficial to my body. We had beautiful weather during the first three months, which absolutely drained me. However, I did not suffer from sunburnt eyes, which I had the previous few summers. I always wore my sunglasses but still ended up with super sore eyes.

Before Covid hit the world, I had just started with a new physio. They aimed to get my pelvis balanced as I carried most of the weight on my right leg, causing me much discomfort behind my right knee. I was fortunate to never incur a large right leg due to this. They also worked on recognising my left leg by the brain as being safe. It was all about rebuilding signals from the leg to the brain. They gave me my homework, and I did it. Practice makes perfect, as they say.

One specific area I worked on during lockdown was my left arm. Having my left arm work with my right side was quite challenging. I worked on strengthening the arm to create stability. The ball and socket in the left shoulder where the humorous bone fitted into the shoulder was extremely loose. There was no stability there for me: no strength and coordination. I would pick something up with the left arm, and it would have a mind of its own. It would shake uncontrollably in the early months, making it impossible to hold anything in my left hand. Later on, it was hard to rely on it; for example, I would make toast, and I could not hold the toast with my left hand while I buttered it using my right. I could not slice fruit for my cereal as I needed to hold the fruit with my left hand while I sliced with my right. It would highlight all the small, simple daily tasks we do, which we do not even realise we use the left hand for; this is providing you are right-handed. After the three-year mark, its unreliability became less consistent. However, it would still be there most of the time, giving me a break occasionally.

I had a kettlebell weight, which I would lift with my left arm. At the start of doing this, I had no control over the arm movement. I would flick the weight out, but with time it became more fluid in its movement, and I could pull the weight up and down with control. It was all down to the signal from my brain to my arm. I had strength in my arm, just no coordination. I could feel the left side of the brain working hard as it would judder about; I never felt the right side. Most of my body was disrupted, and a clean line signal was required so that they could all join up nicely.

Swimming

I always considered myself an okay swimmer. Living on the coast and enjoying the sea, it was a priority of mine to be confident in the water. The first summer of my recovery was 2018, as I came home in August 2017 and didn't really see the remainder of the summer. My parents took me down to the beach as it was too warm being stuck around the house.

The ocean was particularly flat, making it extremely inviting to practice swimming. I was shocked when I realised I could no longer swim. My head was so weighted in the back of the skull it made it extremely difficult to perform any swimming action. My left arm also didn't want to cooperate. When attempting to go underwater, this was also affected; my head felt as though it was filled with helium, encouraging it to resurface instantly. From this experience, the following year, when I was slightly more stable, I went to a local pool, which proved to be quite quiet, which was perfect for me; otherwise, I think I would have been easily discouraged from it being busy. After venturing to the establishment a handful of times, I soon improved my swimming technique; I had a float, which I used to help strengthen my legs by holding it out front and kicking. It felt like the brain remembered and tried to rectify everything it struggled with. My underwater attempts stayed the same and never improved during these immediate years.

During 2020, I started to get tired of the fact that seeing was still a struggle. All the muscles used in using my eyes had a knock-on effect of tiring the brain. It was so hard, and I was starting to experience a low. A friend told me one day, as I shared this hardship with them, I once told them I experienced no emotion... I had to take it on board as a positive that I was now experiencing emotions. If I was sad, as much as it was not nice to experience, I was experiencing an emotion - something I wouldn't have before.

After three years of trying and putting the energy into my recovery, I would have liked some form of independent living by this point; I'm only human, after all, and I felt it was only natural that anyone in my situation would have wanted the same outcome. Yes, I had good days, and yes, I had bad days; I could have done without the bad days, though we all have them; it's like when we say, "Someone got out of bed the wrong side", I'm not talking about my mood, but on a physical level. We can't help it - the body just decides it hasn't got the energy and coordination for the day. The same applies to someone's mood towards the day. So, it can be physical or mental, deciding the day's path.

Simple actions improved after three years, such as getting in and out of bed on both sides. My bed was positioned in the middle of my room, allowing me to get in and out of the left or right sides. I could only get in and out from my right side; my brain would judder viciously when I attempted this simple action from the left. For some bizarre reason, the brain didn't like me using the left side of the bed. After three years, the brain started accepting the left side of my bed, and the juddering faded. It was lovely being able to use both sides of the bed again. An action you wouldn't think you would appreciate so much until it's taken away from you.

Diary Entries: January 2020

I saw myself walk from the parked car outside the establishment to the establishment unaided. It may have only consisted of a handful of steps but it was still an achievement. My inner sway has calmed right down. It would still appear if tired, though overall, it has minimised. This didn't happen often, but on this day, I was aligned.

It was extremely difficult to throw a ball up in the air and catch it again, yet we all do it without any thought. It's automatic, and we never pay attention to the structure we use within our bodies.

My left arm didn't coordinate correctly for the throw and catch, plus my left eye vision was damaged, which would make my left side of the brain hurt. I guess this was because the vision was processed faster due to the constant movements involved. Add this to my non-existent balance with standing, which is quite a complicated equation. Even throwing a ball seated was challenging as I struggled with sitting stable. During my third year, I practiced this action as I had reached a new level of stability. It was good training for me with coordination.

Trying to have others understand the daily hardship and struggle you endure becomes extremely frustrating and disheartening as no one possibly understands, even if they feel they do. For example, this was the case for me when I was trying to achieve activities independently rather than linking arms with someone. I could step out of the car, and others would see me standing as I always have, but it's suddenly forgotten what would be next on my ever-long list of symptoms. I would be standing by the vehicle, unsure about moving as I'm continually swaying internally; moving a footing may make me off balance, and I'd stumble. The back of my brain is playing pinball as it's trying to process all the information. My vision is blurred, and I don't want to move my head too much due to the lack of vision. I must manually move my left leg (talk to it) when I need to move. My right calf hurts, and I must think about everything and converse. It's a lot. When we are ready to leave the vehicle, I'd require solid instructions on where we would be heading, whether left or right. For example, I can't cope with being told to go right and then cut up as we need to go left. The brain has a moment and can't manage the spontaneous information as it's unable to multitask or chop and change. These actions would see me end the task quickly as I simply couldn't manage any of it. I'd attempt these new actions without being link-armed with someone as I required my independence, but I also needed to be stable enough to carry out simple tasks. I had spent thirty-six years full of balance and feeling stable in my daily living. I was not going to give it up yet, as I hoped I had many more years ahead of me for improvement. I placed so much faith and belief into the body that being able to repair and heal it became my coping mechanism. We have designed ourselves from birth, so we must be able to redesign ourselves.

The body is never still. If I can steal ten minutes of stillness from it when I wake in the morning, it's heaven. We naturally take ourselves off to rest and lie down when tired or exhausted. For me, this wasn't possible. My body never went into a still state of mind. I would lie down, and I'd still be internally shaking. It was super upsetting knowing that I couldn't escape the sensations for any time.

I've started noticing my left leg when I am lying in bed. Up until now, I have never really noticed the left leg. I never felt as though I only had one leg; I just did not acknowledge my left. The only sensation I ever really received from the left was a sore heel, cramp and something heavy on top of it when there wasn't anything there, and it became overheated for no apparent reason. I felt something when I moved it, and only now, with the feeling returning, did I realise I had temporally lost this sensation.

I started doing hand weights in my third year. Due to my left arm still juddering and unreliable with its actions, I decided to concentrate on strengthening the signal or rebuilding it as I am unsure of the damage incurred. I'm hoping this helps the cause. I have purchased some 2kg dumbbells and am performing the simple arm exercises suggested on the leaflet that comes with the dumbbells. I'm sure searching online or in a book would also offer suggestions. I felt it would benefit the signal and hopefully help ease the judder. I also borrowed some ankle weights from a friend. I did the same for my left leg in regards to exercise, which was particularly weak and unreliable.

Every day for around three years, I would cry internally. Some would say I had every reason to cry; I was allowed to feel down and sad about the situation. However, when this moment passed, I would again put on my smiling mask, get on with my day, and remind myself that I could do it. In some situations, it was hard to see the light at the end of the tunnel, though I just believed there was one. Even if I couldn't find it, I kept believing there was one, and I wasn't going to show I was struggling to find it. I would probably say my Dad was my biggest fan in helping me achieve my goals. Don't get me wrong, sometimes we did not smile, but we just battled on. I probably laughed at my errors, built that bridge, and got over it. I would call myself the 'pet dog' as I could not leave the house alone or walk without someone with me and assisting me. This was particularly hard. I had lived an independent life, coming and going as I pleased, and now I could do nothing alone.

Daily living became more tiring and depressing. Did I hang up my hat and accept that this is how it is now, or do I continue battling to achieve independence? Of course, I continued to achieve a level of independence. I felt there was more to accomplish before I concluded my new normal. I knew this new life would include new limitations, though I also knew I'd achieve this new life with independence. This was the goal I strived for, and it was my main goal from day one. I would learn to adapt to my hampered abilities. I would see it as an absolute bonus if I regained any of these. If I never regained my tampered abilities, I would learn to live with new limitations.

I was taken to a nearby local city in early 2020 using Park and Ride; I was getting better at using Park and Ride and buses. I noticed that my swaying had calmed down again. Strangers asked me to move from the offered disabled seating on many occasions, for which I refused. I secretly hoped they'd feel guilty for asking me to move when they witnessed me struggle to walk. When stopping in shops, I was not swaying as much as I used to. I could attempt a few steps independently outside shops and within crowds, which I would not have tried on previous visits.

Diary Entry: March 2020

My eyes were showing improvement. My double vision was becoming less frequent. My image was stabilising and would bounce as my brain bounced in the damaged area, but this was becoming less frequent, too. My entire body had taken a step in the right direction with stabilising.

Diary Entries: April 2020

Looking at a tablet, phone, or paper-based reading material is slightly clearer. The second image does not distract me as much, and my eyes do not hurt as much. My vision is noticeably better, but I still struggle with seeing perspective/depth. It is holding out for the entire day, whereas it would deteriorate throughout the afternoon before.

Walking is stabilising and I'm becoming stronger in my skeleton. Positioning - I'm better on the balance board and the treadmill. I'm training myself to place footwear on without sitting. I'm practicing one-legged standing and walking through doorways without touching frames. My left leg still struggles, with judders from my knee, and my knee judders alone at times. I still get pulled left and right by my brain, though this has calmed. I'm placing a lot of weight on my left foot and I can hold a pretend note down under my heel. I'm making the leg recognised by the brain as safe. I'm practising stairs without a handrail. The stairs are enclosed and narrow, so they're safe, and I can manage four steps before I start swaying over. My gait is becoming narrower and starting to feel more natural.

Over time, there were some days when vision was primarily taken through the good eye, which was my right. The left eye was proving to be more of a hindrance. I may not have had it, as I received no recognised vision from it.

It was during April 2020 that I noted I can now walk and move my head around slightly. I can also look down towards my feet when walking, which was impossible for me up until now. This is a sign that something has improved/healed within the brain. I am achieving more and more steps solo. I still have a long way to go with this action, though it is promising that the few steps I can take will become more grounded.

There was still no crying taking place, three years on from the bleed. I would, on many occasions, be crying internally as daily activities would be beyond challenging. Everyone around me would see I was doing my best at the task in play. As I would laugh at my errors, no one actually saw how upset I was that my task was really hard for me to perform. I had a light-hearted banter approach to most of my actions, which may have gone against me as I always portrayed that I was all good, just going about my business in a slightly awkward manner. I couldn't exactly be all sad and depressed about how hard it was for me; that wouldn't be any good for anybody's mindset. Plus, it wasn't me. I already felt a hindrance to everyone who took time for me; I didn't want to dampen the mood.

Head sensations

My brain gets very tired. I've experienced more headaches this past month, all of which have been in my forehead and temples. My neck has become uncomfortable and hurts slightly, as it did in my early days, where the skull meets the spine area.

I experience bad visions of tripping up or falling sideways when my brain becomes too tired. Usually, it's overworked and does not choose to function any longer. Sometimes, I feel I must incur injury to myself to show I genuinely cannot go on with what I'm doing. I'm not sure the people around me genuinely understand that. I didn't, however, take this approach. There were situations where I could have easily given in to the off switch, though I chose to override it every time. I once had no concerns about doing and achieving the task, so I continued having no concerns. There were occasions when I just stopped. I'm no superhero, after all.

Diary Entry: May 2020

I'm struggling more and more with post-stroke symptoms. My walking is extremely hard; it may look from the outside that I'm achieving a form of walking, but on the inside, it's absorbing all my energy. Over the last year, some discomfort has started to ease, giving me hope that it will completely disappear with time. I do a lot of one-leg balance practice, and I've still yet to achieve this accomplishment. Upon doing this task, I noticed the ease of discomfort in my leg.

Diary Entries: June 2020

It's strange how I now look at the world differently. I see people differently.

I'm unsure if it's a fault of mine, but I never let go of who I was before the bleed to this point. Others often say you must let go of who you once were, though I never did. It may have been the mindset which got me to the point in recovery I did. I was still me; I just had a hurdle of mobility concerns to address. I still remember how you got from A to B. It would take me some time to put the actions into play. Knowing how to go up steps was my first tick, as I had this memory which required practice. I was only able to manage steps with a handrail in place. Now, since my bleed, I have realised how important it is to offer a handrail. Coming down steps was equally as difficult as the weight of your head throws you forward.

My eyes feel alien. They don't hurt with strain; they just have pretty uncomfortable feelings. The balance mechanism within my brain feels like it has improved slightly as my inner sway feels slightly calmer. Improvement is very minor, like always, though there are improvements.

I managed an assisted walk out in the wind two days ago. If you took me back a year, you wouldn't even see me leave the house if it was breezy. It would completely drain me. It stems from a visit to the beach in 2018 to watch some surfing at a surf spot that was hardly surfed due to the requirement for a big swell in the area to generate waves at this particular spot. It was quite windy this day. After taking on the weather conditions, I probably took two days to reform some balance within my brain. That day's wind had completely confused my brain, and I paid for it. I was fatigued and struggled to function. Now, when I refer to this struggle to function, it's not in comparison to how I used to use this term/statement. Those days have passed. This new functioning I would experience would be directed at the same points but at a more intense level. It had taken me three years from the bleed to stabilise the brain to these conditions.

Diary Entries: July 2020

Taking the two steps outside the kitchen door into the kitchen from the garden took three years to be able to step without using the grab rail. I was still too unstable to go down them without using the rail. When I refer to being unstable, I refer to being with poor balance, I lean with the foot I'm stepping down with. For example, if I take my first step with my right foot, I will lean out to the right, which would undoubtedly end in a fall. I was well aware of my unstable motion, so I was not a risk-taker. I had learnt my lesson in my first year of recovering where I chose to just step down some steps and fell. In my early months, my brain was in so much denial of what was happening. I believed I could do the same as I did before the bleed. Thankfully, I had a supportive individual with me who saw what I was doing and caught me from head-butting the ground. From this experience, I took a step back and started acknowledging my abilities much more carefully. I believed I would one day be achieving steps again. As upsetting as it was for me at that moment, not alone in scaring my accompanying friend, I did get back up. I knew what I wanted as in achieving my independence along with my balance and it empowered me to fight on. I never wanted to be stranded somewhere and not be able to get from A to B.

I'm becoming less pulled backwards on the step-ups on my step block. Now, my one-leg balance is improving, playing a huge part in making this exercise more pleasant. I'm swaying less sideways.

The sensation of feet on the floor is becoming stronger.

Anxiety has been the most significant disruption towards my recovery. Any kind of anxiety which the body undergoes interrupts its chain of thought. It's a distraction from the mindset set up to achieve its goal - like crossing the road, putting the kettle on, or walking to the table to collect a cup or plate. I'd practice on my treadmill, and if I were trying to hear the radio simultaneously, I'd struggle to achieve the few steps I could do without holding the handle. Due to trying to listen, I was unable to give any attention to my attempted walking.

Diary Entries: August 2020

I was taken out to Portwinkle, a small beach on the other coast, just after Looe in Cornwall. It was this day which saw my first stumble while linked to my Dad. The last section of the walk onto the beach consisted of a small boulder that required judgment to avoid slipping or stumbling off it when venturing onto or off the beach. When leaving the beach, we misjudged the step up off the beach, which only saw us stumbling backwards off the large rock and flat onto our backs. Thankfully, neither of us hurt ourselves to the extent of where we couldn't get up. I'm sure we looked like a pair of drunks if we were spotted by any onlookers. This incident really shook me up, and it took days to regain confidence in my situation. At that moment, it was brought to light just how hard work it is for anyone in my company. You run a little video clip to yourself to remind yourself how far you have come, and even though this precise moment has proved to challenge you, you still have achieved it. I always felt like I was in a movie where situations like these would arise. This was not our first stumble outside in the three years post bleed, but we had done pretty well. It wasn't the best way to end a beautiful day at the beach. No, that was when we got some local fish and chips and watched the sunset.

I had a new shin sensation on my right shin that felt like a metal rod as it was strangely heavy. It gave me a warm sensation and slightly throbbed. It has been happening for a good year. Putting footwear on without wall holding or sitting is somewhat improved.

Diary Entries: September 2020

As emotions and feelings returned, I struggled a little bit more. Every action taken within the day was effort. I was starting to reward myself with more and more rest days. I recognised that I needed to prioritise my daily activities. I couldn't complete all the tasks like I would have before the bleed. Even though at times I tried, it awarded me the "overdone it" card. I had to pick and choose and then recognise where a complete rest day would be required. It was extremely disheartening and a little depressing at times. I had to look in my wardrobe and find my smiling mask, so my low mood would not affect others. I didn't want the "pity" card or "we feel sorry for Jo" comments etc.

I was continually moaned at if I was to write any notes towards my book. Thirty minutes on the tablet/computer would leave me with bright red, strained eyes, making me unable to look at any screens for a few days. They would hurt quite bad, almost like I had scratched the lenses of the eyes. It was not all bad, as I would have a reason as to why I couldn't do things days after.

I encountered my first morning waking, where everything was still - with no shaking or swaying within my body at three years post-bleed. My stepping off the bed was better as I was not getting drawn forward to the floor.

When standing from sitting on the beach, my left leg is more stable. Walking on soft sand is still challenging, though I can do a handful of steps unassisted. This is evidence of my balance improving. We all know how unstable soft sand is for walking on, accompanied by unforeseen holes created by individuals digging or digging dogs. Staying on my feet when faced with these obstacles is evidence of improvement.

I often must wait upon standing after sitting for periods of time for the signal to register from my legs to my brain. I'm not very in control of leg movements when first standing.

Type rope balancing is improving due to one-leg balance improving. I am noticing how much one-leg balance is involved in this balance exercise.

When walking on the treadmill, the left foot feels less and less discomfort - it's starting to sit flatter when taking a step.

When lying flat, I experience times when my body is actually still.

I feel the cerebellum throbbing which generates a throbbing sensation in my legs. The left side of my head still has episodes where it's extremely heavy and weighty, controlling me to vary left.

My walking has improved slightly more. My legs are becoming less rigid with steps taken.

The brain is still unpredictable. I still experience that if it doesn't want to know, it simply doesn't want to know. It literally switches off on me. It's almost like I have switched the switch off. However, the brain is clever enough to do this all by itself.

When walking upstairs, the sway has calmed to a minimum. I practice daily but still need a rail to do a flight of stairs. The left leg is still alien to the body. I must manually help it walk. It is becoming stronger only at a very slow pace.

One-leg standing has taken a step forward. I'm managing this action with less worry of toppling over. The left knee has good episodes where it's strong and bad episodes where it offers no support and judders me about.

Lifelong recovery

I was at a routine follow-up, checking I was still on the correct road; the only difference on this visit was that I was hearing a lot of improvement usually comes to an end when the person is three to four years post-bleed. Unfortunately for me, as upsetting as it was to hear these words, I refused to accept them. For starters, I had no independence; I still couldn't take myself out; I couldn't use any form of public transport, not even a mobility scooter, with my damaged vision; I was baffled as to how others expected me to live. I always felt it was all well and good being the individual stating these facts, however, I would always think to try being that individual to whom you are telling the information. Do you get a handout with "how to" on it? No, you get offered nothing; it's just a thank you for coming. I knew I wasn't the only individual who had ever been in this situation and was sure there would have been many alike. As an individual, I wanted to help others who may find themselves similarly. Just being informed of this information does not mean it's correct. They usually tell you nothing as they can't commit to advice. Either way, being told nothing or simply being told you gave it a good shot, but it's time to hang your coat up is not what you'd choose to hear. Theoretically, they can't say anything right, so it's probably why they say nothing.

Diary Entry: October 2020

During this month, I found myself struggling. I was in a low mood at times because everything I wanted to do required so much energy and effort, and my right leg was extremely discomforting. I don't think the COVID situation helped me because the constant mask-wearing within stores made my attempt at getting from A to B that much harder. I struggled enough to attempt this action without the use of a mask. I would make more errors than I would tell people. I quite often found myself spinning around in a circle for no apparent reason or bashing into doorways, which resulted in hurting my arm. It was painful for me, both mentally and physically. Why did I act in this manner? It just happened.

Diary Entry: November 2020

Year 2020 saw my landmark birthday of forty. I always wished to celebrate this one as I was never one to really celebrate birthdays. Due to my poor mobility and the COVID situation, I had to step away from it. I didn't write it off completely; I just postponed it. I will show concern when the world settles down, and I've improved that bit more. Whoever stated life begins at forty may have been onto something. I walked slightly better, swayed slightly less, and acknowledged my balance as slightly better. Basically, everything I did was slightly better. I'm only speaking a few per cent in the grand picture, though a few per cent was better than no per cent.

Diary Entry: December 2020

I have noticed that I now wake in the morning without mucky eyes. Every night for the past three years, I would place clear water eye drops into my eyes to lubricate them from the day. They would sting when I put them in because they were so dry. I would often wake with stuck-together eyelids and excessive eye gunk. Was my eye condition starting to take a turn?

During 2020, I was prescribed some medication to trial in the hope it may address the internal shaking which I constantly experienced. The medication helped in the strangest of ways. I still encountered internal shaking, though I could do my required actions to alongside this sensation. I was double taking my movements. For example, it seemed the swaying sensation was still occurring, though I could perform an act to correct its occurrence. I was hoping that the long-term results would be that I would become more competent around the sway and that the brain would eventually release it, and I would no longer experience it, or if I did, it was minor.

On a positive note, I noticed my legs have calmed in their shake upon standing from sitting. This was brought to light when I was lying in the sun one day in my garden, and I stood up, and my legs were shaking quite a bit. It occurred to me that I hardly ever experience this sensation anymore.

Towards the end of the post three years after my bleed, I felt as though I had reached a roadblock towards my exercises/ rehab. I didn't feel I was improving with them; they were just as hard. When I analysed the situation, I saw that I had improved, though in a different light. It was true I had hit a roadblock, though my overall walking, daily movements and overall posture/stance had improved. I had become stronger, and I didn't recognise any of it. I can quite confidently say I wasn't defeated by not achieving good results the first time. I would stick to whatever the exercise would be until I could do it. This wasn't a case of sticking with the exercise for days; it was a case of sticking with the exercise for months and years. I ensured I stayed in my pyjamas as this encouraged me to stay in rest mode sometimes; I knew that as soon as I changed out of my pj's, I would be encouraged to perform my selected exercises. I may not had been improving on my exercises though I had stepped forward in my recovery. I had to acknowledge and inform myself of this.

Diary Entries: January 2021

This month, I had stabilised slightly in my sway, enabling me to take steps slightly better and making my link-armed walking more stable. My one-legged standing was becoming more comfortable; I could still only manage a few seconds, though I did it with more confidence. Putting socks on without holding on or sitting was becoming more natural; it was still not achieved with speed, though I could do the action, which was an improvement from a year and a half ago when I started practising it. I can step out of the car and take a few steps to join my company, which I was unable to do before as I had to be helped immediately out of the car. I'm more stable at managing the few steps upstairs without a handrail. I'm able occasionally to step on and off my balance board.

I'm more and more aware that I'm only going to heal when my brain chooses to. I continue my exercises and out-and-about behaviour and keep all actions in place with repetition for when the brain is ready. As disheartening as it is, you must stay strong. I was in a lot of mental pain as working the injured area of the brain triggered juddering sensations, which triggered emotions, and all I wanted to do was cry, but I couldn't perform this emotion. I was in pain, and it was not something my company could see. For the first three years, I would laugh it off and keep my smile and morals high, and then, after this period, I started to become more frustrated with the situation. I started speaking up on how I couldn't do it. I can imagine it was confusing for my company to look at me. I was me, the girl with no mobility limitations or sight issues - which was completely untrue.

My sight felt stronger; the double vision lessened, and I could judge distances slightly better. My perspective had improved. I don't struggle as much to place a cup onto a coaster, and I can lean forward to collect something from a worktop or put something down. I can sometimes see pavements and sometimes the difference in terrain. I would usually map out my terrain by shadows. It made the image better but was not great, all of which was extremely hard to achieve before.

I am walking around home and through doorways more easily - not holding on as often for support. I can leave the bathroom without touching the walls, which is a massive improvement. To start, I would guide myself in and hold the wall-mounted heated towel rail, which, of course, was not switched on for support.

It sets my emotions off, and I experience an overwhelming sensation when I lay on the crunch device doing my crunches. However, I do not show emotions due to the readjustment in my brain makeup. Something within the movement releases chemicals, which makes me feel extremely sad. It's the only time this has happened to me.

I would hit stages within my recovery where my struggles towards the day were that much harder. I always believed I was improving, though I sometimes hit pockets where my daily struggles were heightened. These times would place me on the path of 'Why do I bother?' After some rest I'd be back on the path of 'I'm improving.' I always tried my hardest to soar above these episodes as hard as it was most of the time. I couldn't live an independent life, and this was my drive to continue moving forward. I did not understand how I would go about my daily living where I was currently at. Even though I may not have physically been doing something, I was mentally; I didn't really rest my brain as it was always hungry for receiving information.

Diary Entry: May 2021

I fell off my exercise step today and face-planted the floor. The brain decided enough was enough and packed up on me, sending me into a frenzy. I didn't feel tired, but my brain must have been tired due to it being the evening. I would need to have a cut-off point as to when I stop with my home exercises. I was thinking of exercising up to 4 p.m. and then stopping.

Diary Entries: September 2021

We saw a few warm days at the start of this month, and it was good enough to venture to the beach. The sea was flat, and the crowds had calmed down, making the beach venture more pleasant. This allowed me to practice going in and out of the sea without help with walking against the moving water. I walked in the opposite direction of the sea lapping onto the shore and with the sinking sand underfoot on every step taken. It was the first time in four-plus years that I managed it. Don't get me wrong, it was only a handful of steps, but I did it alone, given there were no waves to push me over or many people to distract me. I just looked at the situation as I did it - I walked those few steps into and out of the ocean. I had a glimpse of independence. Yes, I achieved it awkwardly, but I had achieved it. I could only hope it was the start of more independence. If I could achieve this, then surely it would only get better.

I was becoming more independent overall. If we were out in an establishment and I needed the restroom, which we would be positioned near, I could go about it alone; I no longer needed someone to walk me over to them. I still suffered from a spinning brain with unpredictable movements, and it was quite unsettled most of the time. I would push it to be independent with its actions, it had to learn not to rely on support.

I became more confident in my approach to situations. I feel this new confident me was released due to my balance improving.

Diary Entry: December 2021

I tied my hair back continually for three years as it would distract my chain of thought too much towards walking if flicked into my face. I was very good at being distracted by my hair and could only attempt actions with my hair tied up. As the years passed and my balance improved, the hair distraction decreased. I attempted walking independently through my garden one day, and my loose hair blew across my face; my brain didn't freak out and panic, and I just continued walking. It was at this point I noticed the improvement. I wouldn't take this for granted and attempt everything with my hair down, but I would slowly introduce the hair-down approach.

You must put the work into physical recovery, or you will waste away; muscles will not strengthen, signals within the body will not rebuild and reconnect, plus balance will struggle to even itself out. Stepping on and off pavements, I began achieving this with little thought. I would practice stepping on and off my aerobic step block, which would still incur unwanted brain sensations, causing me not to achieve the simple stepping-on and off-action. Continually doing this action has enabled me to step on and off pavements, and I don't understand why, but this happens without the brain pulls. In my example, I'm showing that repetitive exercises pay off, though they sometimes reveal the outcomes in a different form rather than the exercise itself.

I had to be particular in what I could participate in as I struggled with my balance, mobility and vision. Taking part in activities aimed at fifty-plus was best for me as I couldn't participate in high-impact activities. I had to be helped in many classes, and all the other participants always accepted me. At the end of the day, I was different from them. I was not the correct age to join the class; I walked awkwardly, my balance was poor, and I had to concentrate loads to see correctly. Despite all this, no one treated me any differently.

Symptoms fading

During my fourth year, I acknowledged how I was still struggling with my daily actions, though it felt as though they were fading. I had been struggling so intensely with my symptoms that to sit at a table to drink coffee on occasion with a friend who has taken me out and been able to see my company was a major improvement. This was due to my eyes slightly improving and being more stable, where I don't sway and am able to actually pick my spoon up to stir my drink without knocking table accessories.

In the early morning, I would be very unsteady and have to reach for walls to help with my balance. Also, my head would judder me backwards, and I would receive a very foggy morning brain. Now, I was noticing all these a bit less.

I was four years post-bleed and was offered an opportunity to participate in a five-day camping venture. My physio at the time offered to take me and assist me throughout. I was super anxious about it as before my bleed, I would have jumped at the idea of a camping adventure; now, with my many deficits, I pondered the what-ifs. I saw the situation as this: I live my life on a line; below the line are my family and friends, whom I'm always in the company of, so they're my comfort and support blanket. Above the line is the unknown; when I step into the unknown, my support blanket will pull me back to the line as I fear danger. If my support blanket is removed, I'd have to step into the unknown and deal with it. This is what the five-day venture would offer me. It may be just what was required to see me branch into the next stage of my recovery. Removing my support blanket may help me improve my progress compared to the current project, as I have to work a bit harder.

Unfortunately, this camping adventure never took place, as someone later suggested that it was a bit advanced for a group of brain injury survivors. Camping is quite challenging when abilities are altered.

I remember seeing this tv programme where an individual had to walk up a lane to get to this particular house; only when they had reached the house, they needed to venture up a flight of steps which I noticed had no handrail on offer. These highlighted situations would encourage me in my recovery. I didn't want to be the individual who couldn't get to the house due to all the steps. I was back in the stranded boat. No, I wanted to be the individual who overcame all my obstacles. These scenarios would encourage me to practice stairs and steps without using the handrail. I was extremely fortunate that my home was laid out the way it was, enabling me to practice within a safe environment.

I can put all the practice into my recovery, but improvement only appears when the brain is ready. I never knew when improvements would show. It took years of being repetitive in my ways.

It was no longer the inner body sway hindering my balance performance but the actual balance mechanism within the body. I couldn't balance simply because I had very little balance. Up to this point, I would have suggested that the inner body sway I constantly received was my hindrance to balance. Now, it was simply down to having poor balance.

My teeth were still clasping at 4+ years. The gap between the front teeth hurts the gums, and I cannot bite food using the front teeth. It is very uncomfortable. It feels as if there is a cut on the inside of the gums on the gap, though there isn't anything.

My treadmill was extremely helpful in my recovery.

Up to this point, being 2021, I had experienced that physios didn't confidently know what to do with me. I did not find one who truly understood my symptoms. No one could grasp the unsettled brain sensation and the weight at the back of the skull controlling my balance. Their best option is to treat you as a stroke patient, only I wasn't solely a stroke patient, and though I shared a few similarities, I wasn't a stroke victim. My uncontrollable inner swaying was a symptom that hindered my exercise and practice. Goals took a good six to twelve months to start showing any improvement in the right direction towards achieving the goal. No one really understood my daily concerns and the struggles life was now holding out for me.

I had to keep the smile going; after all, struggles seemed a lot less daunting when faced with a smile. I was adamant that this setback would not beat me. With my positive attitude and consistent determination, I would overcome this speed bump and prove that if dealt this card, don't give up as you can battle it. At times I was very good at leading people into a false sense of security with myself, because I looked as though I was managing the situation. My company would go completely at ease with me only to later being concerned when I made an error. As much as I enjoyed physio help, I found they never really understood what I was contending daily; it felt as though I was very much a grey area for them. Even performing the simplest task could prove to be the most challenging. If the brain didn't want to know, it simply didn't want to know. My physio during 2019 taught me to shift weight onto my heels more as I tended to lean forward. It took a while to get confident about this as I would profoundly get pulled backwards by the head when going on my heels. Also practicing weight shift from side to side. This has loads of unthought-out benefits. The amount we use for the sideways weight shift is huge; it just goes unnoticed.

My main intention with a physio was to correct my walking and balance. I will be to the point in saying that I'm not sure the physios understood my concern. I feel it was pretty obvious that I was struggling. When someone is continually stumbling left and right or unable to move when required on one leg, I think a tailored programme or approach would be beneficial to offer. Not in my case. They treated me the same way as if I had full balance. In one respect, I found it nice that they didn't want to treat me like an injured party, though in the other respect, they were here to help address the problem. Over the years of trailing in the hope someone may have a more desired approach towards helping me, I realised I was in a no-win game. I would take home any exercises I could continue to do and leave them at that.

I learnt that each physio would have new ideas towards balance, for example, in their first couple of sessions. I would enjoy these sessions and take away any new ideas. Then, it always falls back to the same programme as the previous physio I saw. I could keep things in place, such as movements; they always state practice makes perfect, though it would only come together when it was ready to. This is when p&p is required - patience and prayer. This was a familiar term I would come across. When I first encountered it, I thought of postage and packaging, which was inappropriate unless I was being shipped off somewhere magical.

I started to realise that the number of years I had spent on my recovery to this point didn't mean it had been too long and recovery was now impossible. It was more the idea that recovery had been so long and that the learning pattern I had created for my areas of concern that required improvement was going to be harder, not impossible, as I had to break the incorrect pattern to create a new pattern. It was a case of getting out of the bad habits.

The amount of anxiety which drowns you when preparing for an action, which could be being picked up from home by a friend or getting out of the car, is overwhelming. It's simple actions which swallow you up, encouraging your symptoms to explode. I always knew that I was in the public eye once I left my home. Now, it's all well and good for others to tell you no one's watching you, though it doesn't make it any easier. You are still aware of their presence; you are still aware that you walk awkwardly, can't see correctly, and are forever swaying internally. Your balance is so affected that any change in terrain sends you over.

I had dedicated my life to my recovery, which had been four-plus years where you would see me pretty much every day participating in something which aided my recovery. I was by no means in a stable situation where I could go to work or simply meet up with friends to hang out.

I would always remind myself that Rome wasn't built in a day, and I would face the same outlook. Recovery was beyond slow.

No one understood how I had matching symptoms on both sides of my body when my left side was damaged. If my left leg was shaking, my right leg was, too. If my left foot was incurring pain, the right one was, too. It should have only been the left side, though the right side seemed just as affected. Over time, the symptoms started to absorb primarily into the left.

The following things helped my recovery, or at least I found them beneficial over the years:

Balance board
Walking outside with assistance
Treadmill
Aerobic step block
Home balance exercises- straight line balancing - heal/toe
Seated exercises on YouTube
Standing exercises for seniors on YouTube
Gym
Swimming
Jumping on spot
Hopping on spot
Stretching, floor yoga
Dumbbells
Gym ball
One leg balancing whilst holding the worktop
Tablets for vertigo to help with spinning brain sensations
Frosted lenses to help the double vision or patch the left lens off
FES device for helping left leg movement
Knee brace to help left knee judder
Every vitamin possible in my early years post-bleed to help the body heal

Physios to help with balance and walking
Hydro pool in the early years to help with balance
Visited MS centre to use their Neuro team in the gym
Yoga
Trampoline with assistance for balance
Repetitive home exercises for strength and flexibility
iPad word puzzles for brain stimulation

Six years post-bleed
Active 50's exercise class
Parkinson's group boxing class
iSight art
Local social group
Pub quiz
Coffee out
Gym occasionally
Glasses - tried to black out the left eye

Just because I have a good day doesn't mean the symptoms have eased. I can have a phase of good days, and then I'm back to struggling, and it's like the good days never happened.

Back seat passenger

I used to find being a permanent backseat passenger quite disheartening. In my early months post-bleed, it was a blessing with my damaged vision. As the years passed and my vision slightly improved, being a backseat passenger became quite demoralising. I wanted to see my surroundings, but I struggled to understand my whereabouts in the back due to my damaged spatial awareness. Being unable to see as the others could was quite challenging. I was nearly seven years post-bleed, and on the odd occasion, I would sit up front, but it would really tire me out from my vision. I would get double vision quite badly and would block off the left eye of my glasses, so I was okay. So, in all fairness, I was probably better off sitting in the back.

Sitting

If I sit for any time, I struggle with my balance upon standing. I can't walk comfortably - not that I ever do - but on these occasions, it's particularly bad.

Temperature

When attempting any exercise, if I get too warm or cool, it plays a major part in my actions. It will quite easily upset the brain and cause a sideways-pulling sensation.

People would find it fascinating how I would rock back and forth and control it, so I did not fall over. It was not exaggerated for what I was contending; it was really happening. It may have looked fascinating to others, though it was taking a toll on my mental state. Being challenged by these events is really hard to control. Of course, I don't want to fall, and I don't wish to need constant assistance to help stabilise myself. I require the brain to learn to do it. This action was automatic before the bleeding. I'd never experienced this condition before, so I believed it could be automatic again. I believed so much that the brain was going to heal itself pretty much to where it was before the bleed happened. I also believed it was going to be slightly better than before, as I had a new outlook and understanding towards the world around me. I also gained new knowledge of the biology of the human body. Not everyone experiences the sensations of bone connections, muscle connections, and movements like I do now.

I achieved sit-ups on my crunch device most days, and it was only after around six-month blocks that I could increase the number I would aim to achieve. I would do leg raises, too, which I hoped would help strengthen my lower abdomen. I couldn't place both legs together when raising them as my left leg would judder away, and it always had a mind of its own. After a year of doing these weekly, I could hold and raise both legs. My core never strengthened how I would have expected. Nevertheless, I did see results that gave me the extra enthusiasm to keep doing what I was doing. To keep up the initial enthusiasm for as long as I did was a result in itself.

Activities such as kayaking, cycling on a trike, walking netball, wall climbing, etc, were more beneficial to my recovery than standard repetitive exercises. As much as repetitive exercises are beneficial, introducing sporting activities encourages decision-making and coordination to take place. They challenge you cognitively. These activities would, of course, be altered to your abilities as my balance and non-independent walking would cause problems.

You become so grateful and appreciative of anyone who gives you the time of day, whether they are the happy individual paid to sit behind the desk or who assists you within an establishment. Either way, if they treat you like a human being and see past your troubles, they are good humans.

A good gauge for monitoring my improvement was the ease of entering the bathroom from my bedroom. The rooms were located next to one another. As time passed, I used the walls less and less for support, which showed me I was improving.

Trying to stand from the floor could only be achieved if I went on all fours first or if I was pulled up. I couldn't rock myself forward into a standing position.

I was into sixth year post-bleed and still struggling with my walking/balance/vision, to name a few. You are correct in thinking symptoms did ease up, though they never entirely went. Symptoms have good and bad times. You feel like an improvement has happened, and it reverts to its old struggling self. You must stay enthusiastic and positive and not let the setbacks dishearten you.

Finding financial help was extremely difficult, and no one understood me. Yes, I had use of my legs, as in I wasn't paralysed. Still, walking was extremely difficult, and I had all the other symptoms I have mentioned.

Now, all this has been a huge challenge to my everyday life. I would be unhappy as I wanted to go to work and have money, but in a realistic light, what could I do? My walking wasn't up to scratch, and I often required assistance; my balance was weak, and I could easily fall. I couldn't do stairs very well, so I would always require a handrail and a clear pathway; I couldn't carry items when walking due to my balance, and my vision wasn't strong and my eyes became extremely tired quickly; I couldn't look at any computer screens for too long. My left arm didn't really have any strength, and I became exhausted quickly. No matter how hard I thought about what work I could do, I wasn't strong enough for it. I was like a prisoner in my own body. The mind wanted to live a normal life, but it was physically impossible.

Because I move slowly due to my balance, I miss out on eating hot food. If I have attempted with a watchful eye, to make myself something, by the time I have dished it up, got it to the table, and sat down, I have probably missed the hot food window. It would be more warm food. We take these simple tasks for granted as we don't think about the time taken on them.

Try walking five steps in my shoes and tell me it's not that hard. This was the best example I could offer to help people understand the seriousness of my situation. I was not being lazy, and the people who knew me should know I was not being lazy. However, people could not grasp the idea that I could not do something. It was always "Go on, just a few more steps. You can do it," when, in fact, I really couldn't.

I don't think I have accepted the new me even after six years; the struggle every day offers aren't a way of life.

"The only way to move forward is to actually move forward."

Jo Ulczak

Chapter Eight

You Only Knew a Part of Me... Which No Longer Exists

Even though I was saved, a part of me died that day of the bleeding. Everybody wants Jo back, but I will never be that girl again. I was a free spirit surfer who came and went as and when. Maybe I was never supposed to exist from now forward? But I have, and by doing so, I will share my knowledge from the brain bleed in the hope it helps another. Nevertheless, I have changed.

Do you forget who you were? No, you don't forget who you were, but forget the ease of daily living. You forget over the years how easy it was to walk about, how nice it was to take yourself off on a walk or to participate in a form of activity. You forget how nice it is to pop out in the car to watch a sunset, for example, because you haven't driven for so long or had the independence to achieve this. You forget how nice it is to ask friends to meet you for coffee or lunch as you can't walk about independently. Suppose you do meet with friends for a catch-up over dinner. In that case, they assist you - and you have forgotten how easy it was to walk through the establishment to the table as the new normal for yourself involves an awkward walk accompanied by assistance and awkward mannerisms. Eventually, you mould into your new self. It happened over time; a lot of time had passed before I became this new version of myself. I was not mentally different; I just had mobility and vision concerns, which the brain tried to adapt around. For example, my double vision never dispersed, but I was no longer acknowledging it as much.

A brain concern can be just like any other bodily concern. For instance, you cut your arm, which can be minor or major. If the brain concern is minor, there is a chance of very few symptoms to follow. Also, the location of the bleed is important for the symptoms you will incur, just like a cut. If it's minor, you just put antiseptic on and place a plaster on it. If it's major, then more procedures will be required. This is exactly the same for brain injury.

Life wasn't mapped out for me, which involved a brain haemorrhage along the way. It has taken years away from me and my family and friends. It's not only myself who is affected by the situation, as it affects anyone connected to me. Life does not always pan out the way we intend it to, but that does not mean it's not going to be a good one. My life is still going to be good, it's just going to have a new ending to the original one I dreamt of. However, that's not a bad thing. It may even result in a better way of life; one I would never have dreamed of.

I never forgot who I once was. I had a full set of memories that shaped my former existence. I didn't want to forget; it was a part of me that existed for the first part of my life. I've now reached a new chapter and a new version of myself. Writing my notes was my way of expressing my experience. What the body was experiencing was fascinating to me. It was overwhelming how much I was learning about our body's make-up. It was a life lesson unique to me. It was a life lesson that no one else would understand due to not experiencing it.

As time went on, I became less prominent in my way of thinking. I was settling into the new way of life. I accepted that I don't need to live daily like I once was. I accepted that my life goals were now slightly altered and that I had new goals. I accepted that my abilities may now be slightly different. For example, 'I may now only be able to walk upstairs using a handrail and not run'. I would never aim to look at my new outcome as less convenient but just as a calmer view. Maybe I was too much in a fast lane and needed to calm down. I would have to look at my situation and take all its positives. Even if they seemed far-fetched, I would still use them. I was never going to have this experience and take nothing from it. How would humanity learn from this experience if I never expressed it? That being said - every experience is absorbed differently. This experience is only how my body dealt with it. However, if anything, it will show that a brain haemorrhage is a battle for anyone to tackle, and staying strong and positive is your best friend through it all.

I will probably look at my book in years to come and wonder what I thought when I wrote this. Only everything is so apparent in the early days. There's no middle ground - it's either yes or no. They say letting go and accepting the new you is the way to move forward; only I still felt like the old me before my bleed, even three years on. I still lived for long coastal walks, surfing, playing tennis, going out on my pushbike, etc. It's not that I was able to do any of it. I had not yet settled into a new me. I had no independence to mould into a new me. After three years, I realised the new me would still be me; only I would now have new limitations; it was more a case of moulding into this individual. I was reading into this statement of letting go of the old me all wrong. For me, the injury hadn't taken away who I was. It was more a case of providing me with new limitations to my abilities.

Good family and friends get you through the hard times - they really do. The people who have remained dear to me through this episode will stay with me forever.

It's lovely to hear people tell you that you're doing really good, but it's frustrating at the same time. So much effort goes into every movement you do. Everything is tiring; everything is hard work. Living every day like this is enough to just make you want to give up trying to reach the end result. When people say, "You're here, aren't you? You're alive", you question whether it's all well and good and if you enjoy it. If life is now just about staying strong to get through the day, that's not living in my eyes.

I had to live each day as if everything was fine. Yes, it was super hard and upsetting, but I had to wear a mask and show that I was fine. I would go and see friends; I may not have been able to see them correctly due to my vision, though I would still go and visit. I would have to be walked in and seated at the destination as I could not do this task without assistance.

My quiet self was the version that existed for the first part of my life. Now, it will no doubt see me speaking up a little more. I had lived in the shadows for a good thirty-six years. It was time to have my say, and I started with this book.

As the years passed, my prominent attitude slowly eased away, and my compassionate line would slowly come back into play. I was very black-and-white with my opinions in my early years of recovery. I think due to the trauma which the body encountered, giving people the benefit of the doubt was suddenly overrated. Life was too short to sit on the fence to wait and see. The answer was either yes or no. As time went forward, I slowly brought compassion back into the way I made my decisions.

My automatic mode has gone; I'm only on a manual drive. Everything I now do; I have to tell myself rather than just get up and go as I would have before my bleed happened. For example, if I'm sitting at the table having a cup of tea or a meal and someone asks if I wish to pop out in the car, I must calculate my actions involved in getting to the vehicle from the table, all of which will require assistance. This could be how many steps are involved from the table to the chair across the room where my jumper sits. How was I going to stand from my chair? Am I going to push up from the table, pull up using the back of another chair, or attempt it doing nothing but using my body weight? How was I going to get my legs out from under the table? These are all actions we take daily and never think about. We run on automatic brain power; it's only now that I have this luxury stripped from me and am being resorted to manual power that you see how intelligent our brains are. It was exhausting to get up from the table after consuming much of my energy, and my energy levels would be affected before I left the house. I had first-hand experience with how our brains calculate our actions and store the equations for repeat use. It's no wonder all brain injury survivors struggle with fatigue as much as they do.

Some days, I would just wish to be piggyback-carried everywhere. This didn't happen as medics informed me I wasn't going to get better if I thought like that. I wasn't being lazy; I physically didn't have the performance to attempt walking those few steps unassisted. I would cry within as I knew that I simply couldn't perform the action, and no one was willing to help me. Just because I ask with a smile doesn't make me okay. I would not participate on these occasions, I would sit them out, and answer the many repeated questions about why I chose not to participate. All questions would have the exact same answer: my body can't participate without assistance. I believe people thought I was being dramatic and weak when asking for help. Everyone requires help with some things in life, and this was mine.

If no one were going to take me seriously, then I would just sit and watch or stay behind. On my hand, I would feel I was being hard, and on my companion's hand, I was maybe seen as a slight hindrance. At the end of the day, I wanted to see everyone having fun and freedom; they didn't need me holding them up. As hard as it was, I accepted it over time. It took years, but I got there. I knew that these individuals took time out to do things with me for which I could manage, and some even spent time with me, allowing me to attempt free walking. Keeping me involved is invaluable, and I don't easily overlook it. I knew I was hard work and awkward in my ways, so to have individuals give you the time of day was priceless. They knew I would become their responsibility when in their company.

A&F

"I'm exactly where I'm meant to be."

Unknown

Chapter Nine

The Mask That Always Smiles

You have to wear a mask to the world during this temporary period and mask away the actual pain which is involved. Every time I leave the house, I wear a mask. I must show spirit in what I do. I must cancel out everyone on my path to achieve the few required steps. In the early days, I achieved this with much assistance, and in time, I completed it with less help. Though both efforts needed the mask. Knowing my walking was now different in its stride meant that others would note me. If I were to acknowledge everyone who may look my way, and no, it was not for my good looks, I would not be achieving any goals I had. If I were to shy away due to individuals going about their day and being in my path, I would not be where I am. People don't know or understand how much effort goes into a single step. I only know this through my circumstances, which may only be relevant to myself. However, it may be extremely like others who come to find themselves in similar situations.

Not only am I wearing this mask to see me attempt activities, but I also wear it to show I'm dealing with the situation okay. Really, I'm struggling; I'm crying, and I'm in pain mentally and physically; I want it all to ease away, though I can't show that; well, I could, but then it would be 'poor Jo.' I want to be treated as a human, not a piece of cotton wool. As time passed, it was proving to be a case of 'I looked good, so I must be good'; little did everyone know the struggle it was just for me to stand. No one knew all the symptoms I was contending. It wasn't me to stand there and share all my demons for that precise moment. I remember how I would stand and shake vigorously on my legs in my first year; it made going out and about assisted nearly impossible. This eased with time, though it took years to calm to a minimal.

The word **stare** jumped out at me, and I found this was a common factor where my presence was noted. No onlooker would understand what was going on with me. Was I drunk? Was I just rude and ignorant when I bashed into them in passing? Did I just ignore everyone's existence who may have been in my radius? No is the answer to all questions. My vision was damaged, which resulted in me not seeing your presence. I also concentrated all my energy on my walking, which resulted in me being unable to acknowledge anything or anyone around me. The brain was unable to multitask. If I bashed you, it resulted from having no perspective on my vision, meaning I could not judge your distance from me. I was very popular with walls, too.

It was difficult to have individuals understand my symptoms. Because it can't be seen like a broken limb or a cut, it's extremely hard to treat. Was I making it up? Oh, how I wish I was. Every day was the same as the day before. I would only notice the improvements when I looked quite far into the past.

'I am meant for better', was a sentence that would repeat itself. I had all these challenges, and I hadn't even reached forty. I was not the only candidate challenged; there were plenty more. Some would be older and others younger, their obstacles and challenges would be personal to them. This may highlight the loss of a limb, paralysis, neurological troubles like mine, or adapting to using a wheelchair; the list is endless. These new adaptations should not be received as a new loss of who you were but looked upon as a better who you are now. You are greater than in the past as you now have more knowledge and understanding. You have achieved a better you. Of course, this has been a path you had never dreamed of mapping out, though it is always said you don't always get what you wish for. It was this way of thinking that helped me over the years. It may not be correct for you, but I had to change the whole situation into a positive in my mind, talk to myself as if I was writing a book, and mentally make notes of my achievements, no matter how small they were. Acknowledging all my movements and improvements and telling myself well done, it's getting better. It was my way of dealing with it.

I was always strong in my bond with the individual I used to be. It was as if they had never left, and it has helped me through my recovery with my vivid memories of how to make actions/movements. After three years of never letting go, it was as if it was starting to fade away. I had spent so long molding this new individual I am today, which involved seeking assistance where needed, making others aware that I'm a little awkward with mobility, etc., all of which was becoming an automatic reaction to situations, that this was becoming my new version. I guess it's from this point that I started letting go of the previous version of myself and accepting the new version. All new ways of life were becoming natural; they were not alien, and that's how I would go about my day now. I'm guessing this is when they state you must accept the new you. For me, it appeared gradually over the years. I didn't set out one day with a purpose. I had heard the term "accept the new you" throughout my recovery and never really took it on board, as I guess I never wanted to accept it. I was me, and I will return to me again, was my mindset. Which I did to some extent, I just had new limitations. This being said, I don't think I ever accepted the new me. As much as I wanted to, I just couldn't.

I never wanted to forget what I could achieve before my bleed and the person that I was, as I believed it helped me regain some of my disrupted abilities. Over time, it became obvious that letting go of my previous abilities made moving forward that much easier. You start enjoying what you can achieve now instead of judging yourself on what you could do once upon a time.

Putting life on hold was one of the hardest things to do. It's built into us all to have dreams and go forward in achieving them. I had to accept that I was not systematically designed, so my dreams would take a bit longer to place back into the picture. I was scared at times, struggled with low mood, and thought that maybe I would not reach a point where I was comfortable and stable enough to go forward in search of my dreams/life expectations for myself. I had to place this fear aside and rise above it. Be the stronger thought process. I was determined to achieve a comfortable life, which I had accepted would be slightly different from the one I had been living in. However, it did not mean it wasn't going to be a good one. The unfortunate event that had happened to me gave me an understanding of the important things in my path. I would no longer look to worry. Worry would be the thought process that took up much of my energy. My chain of thought was slowly destroying the body without even realising it. I would now only look to all the critical things that have enhanced my picture of life.

Believe - one of the greatest medicines within my recovery was believing I was going to get better. It kept me positive and enthusiastic to reach my goal of independence.

Staying strong - you can't show how much you hurt inside, as that would only break down the people around you. Situations would make me cry inside daily, though I could never tell anyone that; I had to stay positive and get on with the situation as if it was not bothering me too much. Some days, I simply knew I couldn't manage the task ahead. However, I still had to give it my all and show willingness, no matter how much it hurt me mentally or physically.

I went on a caravan holiday, a four-day trip with my parents and brother, about two years post-bleed. I would say it was a huge positive in terms of recovery. This was mainly due to the fact you had to have confidence. I would say this trip helped me progress. I had to do things out of my comfort zone in front of individuals I had never seen before. One thing I took away from the trip was that you really do learn not to take notice of others. My entire life, I had noted everyone's whereabouts when carrying out daily tasks. For instance, I saw everyone in the room and cared how I looked to them. This trip showed me that I had to not worry too much about everyone else in the room; all my energy was to be placed on me alone.

The only way that best suits living with a brain Injury Is to live as best you can to a normal way of living. If I were to look at my situation with a half-empty glass, then I would probably not be here now telling my story. That's evidence of what a positive mental attitude can do.

I would say to myself, no matter how hard a challenge you are contending, as long as you can find a smile, positive endorphins are released, and the situation becomes much less daunting. Smiling through the tough dealt hand only turned it all around into a good dealt hand. I'm not saying this situation of mine or your situation will be fixed by doing this. It helps ease the hardship of it. It's like if you purchased a lottery ticket and got no matching numbers; smiling at the ticket will not produce matching numbers. It will just make you feel less bad for wasting money in taking part. You will be sent messages from smiling at the situation on the lines of 'at least you tried'. You may not be wired up this way, and performing this action has no effect. We are not all connected the same.

"Living is a daily struggle, but its every step closer to the end result."

Jo Ulczak

Chapter Ten | Hard but Not Impossible

I was told by many that I was probably a bit hard on myself. I wanted results and to improve, so I was willing to put in the effort. When I was in my fifth year of recovery, I was finding my efforts hard. My mood had also dropped. To everyone who saw me, I was still smiling Jo, but in my own home, I was struggling Jo. I was exhausted and tired of dedicating my life to trying. There were days I didn't even want to get up because as soon as I stepped off the bed, the symptoms began. I was concerned as to how I was to live my life. My mood had flipped from how it had been wired the past five years of all positives to now being exhausted. Being constantly told I could do it when faced with daily challenges was also mentally exhausting. No matter how much I expressed the situation of 'if the brain doesn't want to do it, it won't', no one would listen. They'd make me do it regardless and usually with little help because everyone thought I would not get better if they constantly helped. If this was true, I'm all for it, but unfortunately, it wasn't. What everyone around me failed to take on board was I had a brain injury, and you cannot override its limitations. I did, however, take the statement on board in a different light in that when someone said it, I'd become upset with frustration, but afterwards, which could be hours later when overlooking the day's events, I would relay the words of "you've got this" and realise I do have it in that I would make something of this misfortunate situation.

I think I've mentioned how I revisit any mishaps I incur. I'm very good at practising what I can't achieve. I'd puncture my pride, but my enthusiasm to try again remained intact. Getting back on the horse, I think, is its motto. No one will ever understand how great a feeling it is to make a step up the stairs unassisted with no sway or shake incurred. It overwhelms you and brings tears to your eyes, not that I could actually cry, and you can experience a stable step. It may be short-lived, but you lived it for that split moment.

Professionals continually informed me I would be different when I made it through this situation. This would freak me out. Different? What does this mean? How was I going to be different? I liked how I was; maybe I could be more confident, though I didn't see this as a massive holdback to my life. I heard stories of personalities changing, abilities changing, limitations, etc. However, you never heard much about the good things happening to individuals. I liked the person I had become; I didn't want change. Unfortunately, it was inevitable that this change was going to take place. I was fortunate not to have my personality changed too much; if anything, I was now more black or white. I did not gain a temper or drown in a mood of intense depression or anxiety. This was evidence that not all individuals who obtain an injury to the brain are awarded one of these. I did have my mobility damaged, which I worked hard to regain but never got it back to what was. I feared being deserted, for example, in the middle of a field and unable to get to the main road for help. I needed to know I was self-sufficient in getting from A to B.

You must leave your dignity behind to move forward. I would be so concerned about who I may see when out that it would hinder my recovery. I'd wake up to the day without my independence when only yesterday I would have been walking the streets. I was no longer the independent individual who everyone last saw. I was now linked-armed with my parents or friends to keep me from falling and who guided me as my vision was disturbed. This adjustment was super hard to get used to in my early months. You must get past the thought of people staring at you as you struggle to walk link-armed with someone. I'm sure it was in my favour that I couldn't see the onlookers due to my vision and just noticed out-of-focus figures.

The new you...

In the beginning, you are in denial about how serious the situation you are in actually is. As time passes, you start to accept the struggle you contend with daily and not care that everyone is looking.

The only person who can help you move forward is you. It's the time and effort which you place into your recovery that shines the greatest results. No one can physically get you walking; no one gets each leg stepping forward in a walking fashion. It's you who does this. It's you who places themselves in the situations which help you to improve. No one else can do this for you; only you can. Others can give you guidance and support and the get-up-and-go motivation, but it's you who achieves the results by never giving up.

When your condition strips away your abilities, you start to feel victimised. I couldn't participate in everyday activities because there may be no handrail on offer where there were a few steps. Maybe there is no ground-floor restroom available in an establishment, or the terrain is super challenging.

The more I sought advice regarding my situation, the more I was informed that I was a rare case. Individuals would openly say they had not come across anyone like me before. This response would lead me to believe no one had survived a bleed like mine before and, therefore, there were no resources for it. Imagine a line: on one side of it is survival, and on the other side is death. I had survived closer to the line than resources and recorded records take you. That's how it was starting to feel anyway.

We all hear about school being the best days of our lives, yet I never really related to the statement. If anything, I sat on the fence with my school time, I never really enjoyed it or hated it. It was only now that I was really understanding the statement. (No worries.) It's a time in life when you do not have to think about anything besides schoolwork and friends.

Life throws us obstacles to overcome, and I could have looked at mine as a ball of depression, the half-empty glass, as I had reached my mid-thirties only to now be physically and mentally challenged. I was unable to enjoy my days. If a form of walking aid could be a solution, I would have taken it. For me, there was nothing. Over time, I came to realise the severity of this bleed, and there was no experience in what to offer or suggest helping my case. It was always the same advice: we all heal differently, and no two brain injuries are alike. I struggled to accept that there was absolutely nothing I could do for myself. I wanted to fix it; I desperately wanted my independence and life back.

I don't feel enough of us who experience any form of head injury document our experience in the hope that it may be useful to help others. We, as humans, aim to get better and move on with life in the best way we can. I have acknowledged this and made it my aim to share my documentation of this experience, which I have endured, to show others that you are not alone; many others can offer valuable information and guidance. You must seek them out. Unfortunately, we don't get an information card when leaving the hospital. How helpful that would be.

If I had written my book in my early days of recovery, it would have been so blunt as to how badly the world was designed to help people with difficulties. I sat back as I saw that I was incorporating this outlook and waited until my mind settled on seeing the world more clearly. I waited until I could analyse situations and understand the outcomes instead of just seeing how bad they initially seemed. This behaviour took patience as all I wanted to do was tell my story. I knew I had to wait before I could put pen to paper. If I wanted to give a realistic account of my situation, I couldn't just dive in; I had to play the waiting game.

The most valuable attribute I have learned from my circumstances is patience. For about six years, I had to learn to be patient to help me through my situation. As anyone would be, I just wanted to make that bit more progress in my recovery, as it wasn't happening quickly enough.

"Look how far you've come," is a common sentence I say to myself. No one stumbles upon achievement by accident. We all must put in the effort after setting ourselves a goal. Why place so much energy into what you wish to achieve only to walk away from it?

It took years before I was strong enough cognitively to piece together my book. As the years went on, my mind became more stable and settled. However, due to my eyes hurting so much and my tiredness, I couldn't concentrate for long, so I could not plan my book in my early years.

Sometimes, life hands you lemons, and you must learn how to make sweet lemonade. It's only as bad as you want to look at it; for me, it was a beautiful, uneven path.

I like to believe that I have achieved the level of recovery through repetitive exercises and the motivation to do so.

I was a floppy mess in the early days. I couldn't even sit upright. I would shake repeatedly as I could only imagine I would if I was suffering from MS or Parkinson's. I had no idea if this was a condition I would now have to learn to live with. I pushed myself to achieve a level of normality, a level of controllable stability. Of course, no medical evidence reports this conclusion; it's only my thoughts on it all from my understanding of the human body.

I have no idea where I found my motivation to continue the path to recovery. It was anything but easy. It was soul destroying. I had strong- souled parents who kept me mentally stimulated, and I would not even notice at the time; only when I looked back on it would I see that if I hadn't done what I had done that day, week or even month, I might not be achieving what I now was. Seeing their daughter endure what life had dealt her was hard for them. And at times, it was pretty unbearable for everyone. But it was the strength of the family that kept my soul alive. I knew in my heart that this bump in the road which I had to overcome was provided to me to see the world in a different light. It was to put me on the right life journey I was to experience. There was never a point where I thought I couldn't overcome this unfortunate event.

I'm no hero in this situation, and I would not like to label anyone who played a part in my recovery a hero. Everyone involved played a vital part, and although it may have seemed obvious that someone helped a lot more than another, every party involved had a vital part to play. My parents were my rock in it all. My Dad was committed to all the physical aspects of my recovery, and my Mum was my Mum - the vital individual who keeps you clean, watered and fed, my sympathetic ear and my coffee chum.

The left side of my brain was the problematic concern. It was pretty obvious as it was on the left of the brain where the bleeding occurred. It felt that the image pathway to the brain from the left eye was blocked, and therefore, the signal was stunned. It would bounce or judder on precipitance and find an alternate route, which created the bounce sensation. It was this sensation that would take control and hinder my attempted walking. Of course, this was my opinion on the situation; it was how the situation would make me feel.

What's kept me strong is knowing individuals have achieved what they believed to be impossible situations. Hearing stories of people who thought there was no light at the end of the tunnel only to keep going until they found it. If you were to see one of these individuals, you wouldn't know the struggles they had endured without being told. These people have shown it is worth all the hardship involved. To look at me, you wouldn't know my daily struggle. I looked as I always do, only now with complications naked to the eye.

I could have gone through my recovery years wallowing in self-pity, or I could have gone through it smiling. I chose the smiling option. It's too easy to feel sorry for yourself; the body has suffered a traumatic injury, which will take time to heal.

Did I want to spend this time thinking of everything and asking the continued question, 'Why me?'

Many of us in the world have endured a severe and life-changing health issue, and I'm sure every one of them has asked the question. When asking that question to oneself, it should be packaged and placed in a box, then asked again differently.

We could say, 'I'm going to come out of this situation so much stronger - it's happened to me, and I'm strong enough to deal with it. We don't all get blessed with this hardship; others must see me as strong enough to contend with it. I can learn and teach from this experience,' and so on.

You might see this as slightly unrealistic, as it's pretty unfortunate that this has happened and that I'm being unrealistic in thinking anything other. However, my understanding is that if we allow ourselves to think negatively, then we have automatically given up on helping ourselves.

Life deals out a lot more hardship to some people than others.

I always kept determination, motivation, and enthusiasm on my side. Without these attributes, I wouldn't have reached where I am currently. Being told in the months after the bleed that it was very much a waiting game on my survival during my induced coma phase, the first twenty-four hours of waking would give an insight into my survival stats, was extremely upsetting and disturbing to my parents. No one knew at this stage what the outcome would hold. It was down to my body to decide how strong I really was.

At the two-and-a-half-year mark, I saw being out and about, becoming stronger with balance. For example, up to this point, I would take myself from A to B in my awkward fashion, and you would only have to blow on me, and it would be enough to send me over. After that point, I could carry out the same challenge in my assisted awkward fashion and wouldn't feel that I was going to topple over with a slight breeze. It was still hard, uncomfortable, and undoubtedly done with assistance, but I would do it. I may not be where I wanted to be at this stage in my recovery, but that didn't mean I wouldn't reach it. I'm sure I could have made it that bit further if I had made it this far through sweat and tears. I had a final goal I had set in my mind, and I was by no means not going to reach it. Yes, it had proved more challenging than expected. I had to turn it into the half-full glass and see the hurdles that I had to pass as exciting, not simply hard work and obstacles trying to stop me in my tracks. This was how I dealt with the situation. I'm not saying it will be right for you; it was right for me, and I programmed my mindset into believing this was my best path. I would always have to remind myself that when I struggled beyond my wants, I'd improved dramatically from when I returned home in August 2017. I couldn't even stand up - never mind, walk a few unassisted steps.

As time went on, I became less concerned with those around me who would no doubt be staring at my current mobility ability. I was accepting the new me. I accepted that the only way to improve was to be seen out and about, moving around awkwardly. The people who mattered all knew of the hand life had dealt and knew that as hard as it was for me, I wasn't giving in to it. I was going to find a stable level of recovery and adapt my life to it. I never believed it would be a bad new life due to being hindered compared to my previous one; it would be a new, exciting journey. If anything, I was one of the few who were fortunate enough to experience a way of living in a different format. There would be people from my past who knew a version of me that no longer exists.

I'd tell myself I was a bit closer to the end result to stay strong and positive towards my recovery. Did I actually know if there was light at the end of the tunnel? I had absolutely no idea, and I refused to think this way. I did not truly know what lay ahead for me; all I could do was believe and have faith that I would reach the goal I had set out to accomplish. All the demons I faced, I refused to let them win my attention. I was going to overcome this situation.

My decision to not participate in events was not only down to how awkward it was for me to participate and the fact I had to rely on individuals for help; it was also due to the fact my body actually hurt. My legs would feel so uncomfortable they didn't wish to be used. My brain would spin in the back of the skull upon standing from sitting, producing a very unsettling sensation within the brain. My eyes would hurt, corrupting my vision. My balance, or rather lack of it, would be heightened.

My age kept my enthusiasm and determination alive. I was convinced I was too young to allow these circumstances to swallow me up. I wanted to spend as much time as possible in my forties in an able manner. I wanted to be someone who made it. The human body is magnificent in what it can achieve. You must believe in it, and it was hard, especially the time it took. Days on end with poor vision, poor balance, poor walking - it was soul-destroying. Everything I had dreamed of growing up had changed. The interpretation of what I had dreamt for my future was no longer. No longer? No, I didn't believe that. It would take me a different route to get to it.

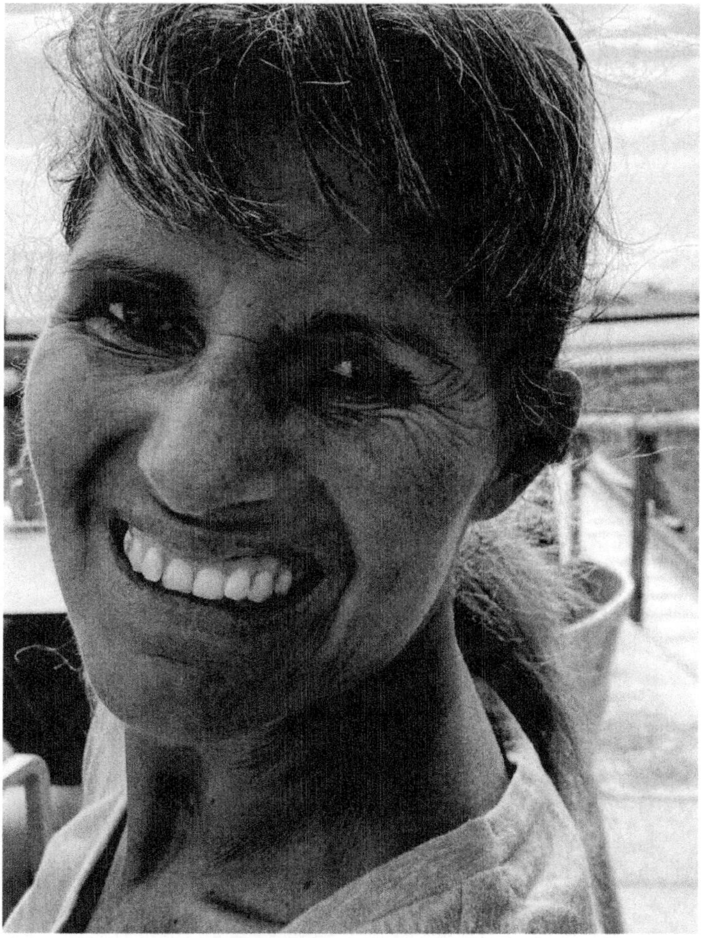

"Everyone hits a low point."

Jo Ulczak

Chapter Eleven

Don't Forget to Cry (Emotions)

It was during my sixth-year post-bleed that I started realising the extent of the damage to my brain. I had always presented that I was doing okay when I was really struggling. I couldn't understand how I was going to live a fulfilling life. How could I work? The bleed had damaged my sight, my mobility and my balance; my fatigue was horrendous, and the area of the brain which was damaged was super uncomfortable. How was I expected to live independently and pay bills? Maybe, in reality, I will never be independent. My chain of thought started becoming realistic to the moment. I was no longer dancing to the tune that I would get back what I lost. I was realising I had to accept the change I had incurred.

When someone asks what your lowest point is during recovery, I find it really hard to answer, as the whole recovery journey is hard and challenging. Do the good days outweigh the bad? Quite frankly, I don't think they do. It makes me question whether I even have good days, as not one day goes by where I think I'm not hurting in any area of my body. I wear this smile, though inside, I'm really crying. I have so many symptoms, which still makes daily living very challenging. If I just had one symptom, I could at least adapt.

So, my lowest point in memory when looking at my life post-bleed would have to be waking up. If I had just passed away, I would know no different as I didn't even know I had been in a coma. This experience post-bleed has made me not fear death. But then I look at the experience and realise that I survived an occurrence which should have ended me. As I mentioned in the beginning, my bleed was deep within the brain, just off the brain stem.

Survival of such an occurrence wasn't a calculated outcome. So why? Or how? It was simply not my time to die, which is the answer. I survived this occurrence to show that the textbook isn't always correct because it says its outcome is negative. I survived to show just how fantastic the human brain is. Yes, it has been very tough and accepting the new me will probably never happen. Adapting to the new me is a work in progress. My biggest challenge is my brain still thinks the way it always has in terms of wanting to be active; I want to walk, I want to cycle, I want to go in the sea, I want to play tennis, I want to get in my car and see my friends etc., only I can't physically do any of this.

I don't have great mobility, I don't have great balance, and I don't have great vision. I am a prisoner of my own body. But this situation doesn't mean I'm now going to live a non-fulfilling life; I'm going to live a different life from the one I had always imagined. Yes, I have concerns regarding my abilities, though new doors have opened, and new friends and acquaintances have entered. These new friends and acquaintances don't know the old me, so they have nothing to judge or compare me to. I can be myself with no expectations. My true friends have continued through life with me, knowing the old me and accepting the new me. They continue to tell me I'm still me who they love to be around, and just because I now have difficulties doesn't change anything. These are true friends. I used to get quite upset when I couldn't participate in events with my friends. This was hard to accept. For example, they could all go off together and do stuff like a simple dog walk, and I couldn't participate. These situations were some of the hardest to accept. I had to acknowledge and accept that they had visited me, so they were still including me, but I had to let them go and be free, something I was no longer. Over time, and it was years, I was more accepting towards these situations. I was always happy and grateful to see my friends who had stayed by me. I had made new acquaintances who would visit occasionally, knowing I was not very mobile to meet them for coffee or a cuppa. Just seeing people would make my day.

Comparing myself to who I was before my bleed was a fault of mine. My brain was so wired up to having the ability to do most things that it now simply can't achieve the simplest of tasks but believed it still could.

It was towards the end of my sixth-year post-bleed that I realised I still hadn't cried. All the emotions I had experienced over the years and the actual traumatic event of the bleed itself, and I still hadn't shed a tear. It was only now that I realised, I had all this emotional journey locked away in a box within the brain. I needed to find it and release its contents to accept myself and the incident I had incurred. My problem was I had to find it.

From looking back at my life journey since the bleed, I recognised that I was in so much denial of the severity of the bleed that I had forgotten to enjoy life. I believed so much that I would restore to the original me that all my efforts went into this chain of thought. I practised every possible approachable angle to aid my recovery. I would be in so much mental and physical discomfort and probably not in a settled brain state to push myself, but I still did. My goal was to be better, and nothing would hinder me. When I refer to my unsettled brain, I'm not just referring to it being unable to cope with the information provided; it was generally dealing with a scramble of information, like an untuned TV.

When I reached my sixth-year post-bleed, realisation had started to set in. My body had become exhausted, my mood had dropped, and I required rest. I slowed down. Towards the end of this year, I realised I needed to cry and let out emotions. My chain of thought was that if I achieved this, I might be able to accept what had happened to me. I was still struggling with me. Everything I did in my day required so much effort, and I never switched off my anxiety. This in itself is exhausting.

As I mentioned in my account, before my bleed, I was an active individual. Since my bleed and my balance became damaged, naturally, my mobility is affected, resulting in me becoming far less active. I had, somewhere along the journey, boxed away the tears of pain that I would have been experiencing regarding this. I was protecting everyone around me to be far less sad regarding my life change, and I now needed to release the tears. I had to seek out this emotion to accept myself and feel my value and worth to move forward happily.

I had encountered and accepted new individuals into my life who, without realising, showed me the enjoyment and kindness of life. I had lost this along my path. What I enjoyed about my new friends was there were no expectations of me. They only knew the new me, the me who required assistance. All my long-term friends knew the original me, the old me. I felt they would forget the idea of me now requiring assistance. For example, we would be out in the car, park and get out of the car. My company would just walk off and forget that I required their assistance.

In contrast, all new individuals in my life only know me to require assistance, which makes them instantly alert and aware of me, never leaving me behind. Yes, I was embarrassed by this, but I had to accept this new me. I had to accept that this was how life was going to be for me from now forward, and letting out the tears was going to help me achieve this. Having my company on automatic awareness was also far less stressful for me.

This particular individual came into my life who, without even realising it, helped me to see life differently. I was shown how to appreciate living and being alive.

My friend was in a wheelchair and struggled with their own daily life challenges, and I would often ask when out, "Don't you get upset seeing the others run around?"

I knew it was upsetting because I couldn't run around either, and seeing others do just that would make me want to participate, but I couldn't. I had to see the world from my mobility scooter, which I had only just introduced into my life.

My friend always replied, "I just remind myself that I am alive".

This response would never really sink in because I would rather not be alive. Why would I, after the constant mobility struggle, balance struggle, vision struggle and brain discomfort? And there's my continual internal sway, which no one knows of as it can't be seen.

It was probably a week from this conversation, and we were enjoying another day out; we were both on mobility scooters known as trampers, which means the rider can enjoy them off-road. I started to understand the reply, "I am alive," as I was with my friend on our scooters. We were on the beach on this particular day with the tide out, and I was enjoying myself. I was enjoying myself, yes. I don't know why the words decided to sink in, but I realised I could still enjoy life. Being around my friend in the same situation as me, requiring a mobility scooter, helped me find my happy smile. I realised being continually around able-bodied individuals was a recipe for sadness. They have no understanding of the difficulties you face mentally. Seeing them nip here and there without any difficulty only results in mental tears for the individual who can't perform in this manner. You feel like a hindrance, someone holding others back when you really aren't. My friend helped me realise this.

I joined a local social group, all able-bodied, which was set up in my town. I was beyond nervous on my first visit due to my limited abilities. How would I be perceived? I had no idea what to expect, but I knew how small my world was becoming, and I needed to brave the world to stop it from shrinking. My parents took me to the meet-up on this particular weekend just before Christmas 2023. It was the best manoeuvre; everyone accepted me, and I made fantastic friends. It took me a couple of months to feel more confident and comfortable with the group. I tend to worry a lot about being a hindrance, but my confidence has improved. I started participating in other events which they participated in. They all knew I required help and were more than happy to help me. There was one particular individual I would confide in about my abilities and how I can be limited in what I can do. They would happily reply that if helping me makes my involvement that much easier and enjoyable, they are happy to help me continually. They never looked to me as a hindrance, or as someone holding them back. They got enjoyment out of helping me. This gave me the confidence to stay with the group. In time, when I knew everyone much better, I discovered this was the case for all others. I was just Jo - who sometimes required assistance and support. My mindset improved, and I became stronger. Joining this group of fantastic people, along with my friend who requires a wheelchair, showed me life's importance. Between them, they showed me what living was like. Before my bleed, I would never have taken this take on life.

I started to accept my circumstances: I would never accept what had happened to me, but I realised I had to accept the outcome. I had to accept I was now disabled with my mobility and that I had left-eye vision issues. I accepted that I didn't need to appear able-bodied to others because I wasn't. It was okay for me to appear slightly different in my ways. I realised people around me noticed I may be struggling and offered me help or space where needed. I saw that people were not judging me; they were genuinely kind. This was extremely difficult to accept. I was now disabled. It still felt like I had no mobility concerns even though I evidently did. However, my life became more manageable once I accepted the new me. This brings me back to my earlier words about people suggesting I accept the new me, but I refuse as I feel I will return to the original me. I understood the statement. I also had to accept the brain sensations my bleed had left me with. I had to accept this was how it was going to be for me from now onwards, having uncomfortable brain sensations and pulls.

Some people may find the example of my feelings extreme. Although that's exactly how I perceived them, it is only an example of how I can express the intensity of it all. I had no feelings or emotions for around the first year after my bleed. Someone could have stabbed me five times in various areas of my body, and I would not have felt any of it. I could have stabbed someone numerous times and not have any emotion in doing so. Of course, I never did this. I would often say, 'My emotional chip has been removed'.

Every situation I encountered was either black or white. There was no middle ground. In some respects, it was quite good feeling this way, as it decreased all the worry and anxiety that comes with caring. Over time, this chip started to emerge again, though it did take some time.

"Be positive, be patient, be persistent."

Murray Newlands

Chapter Twelve

Looking Forward

There's no hiding the fact my life changed drastically in June 2017. You have just read my account of everything I contended daily and am still contending to this very day. Maybe just at a different degree of intensity. This never distracted me from having goals, and if you find yourself in a similar situation where the horizon looks bleak, always have a list of things you would like to do and accept the help you may require. For example, I loved to travel and was more than competent in doing this solo. Now, with my damaged mobility and vision, I would always require company. It's unsafe for me to achieve this solo. In fact, I probably couldn't achieve this solo now - but it doesn't mean I can no longer travel. With my low energy levels, I must be selective about what I do and where I go. I can only manage a short trip as opposed to my month-long holidays before my bleed. If going abroad, I can't choose a destination that takes hours to get to or is known for being constantly hot. I must be choosier and more selective. If wheelchairs are on offer, I must take them because I can't stand for long. My angle with this example is that just because life has dealt you a bad card doesn't mean the outcome is bad. You must look beyond the closed door and see it still has plenty of openings.

Now, when I look to my future after dealing with my many symptoms for seven years, work may be a problem for me. Up until this point in my recovery, I have been very fortunate that my parents have looked after me. I haven't had the stresses of everyday finances to contend with. I pay my way, but I'm pretty convinced my way of living is much less on the wallet than if I were living alone. Though it's no lie, I don't know how I would afford to live on my own. I get basic benefits; as you can imagine, it doesn't go far. I would require someone to live in with me as I am known to fall with my damaged mobility and the brain doing its own crazy thing from time to time. I'd need transport funds as I don't drive, but most of all, I would require an individual to be present with me throughout the day to link me with my walking. Thanks to my parents, they have achieved all these tasks, and I have lived a fulfilling life. I'm not sure how I would have managed without them, to be honest, and it's a bonus that we all get on so well.

So, what am I to do financially? I realise work will now be an issue for me, but at the same time, I need money. I aim to be an inspiration for helping others and to put brain haemorrhage on the map, as I feel it is greatly overlooked. This is from my own experience in seeking advice and guidance. Financially, I'm not sure where it will get me. I'm more driven to help others. I have found writing my book super beneficial, too. It's a way to express myself and offers me therapy in return. Reading over my notes has shown me just how far I have come. It would be really rewarding if it could help another. From doing my book, I have found a purpose to have brain haemorrhage recognised as it is currently not; only strokes are. In the future, I hope to raise awareness towards brain haemorrhages and AVMs. They're serious and often life-threatening, and I feel there needs to be more support towards people who have suffered from them.

Before my bleed, I was in a relationship; after my bleed, I was still in a relationship, but as time went on and the support I required, I found it only fair to be single. We are still good friends, probably even best friends. I always thought that I would be settled down by my mid-forties, but this incident has now changed that vision. Nowadays, I always look at myself and ask, "Who would seriously want to be with me?"

I tell myself, yes, you have limitations, but you have a lot more to you than just your mobility. Do I still think I will have my happy ever after? The answer is yes, I do. Just because something is stripped from you, you are still you. You are you that everyone loves. Genuine people will look beyond your hardship and see you. This is your new life. This is what you have to offer. This is how you must accept your change in abilities. Yes, they differ from before, but you must let that go and appreciate what you can now do. I also feel I will genuinely appreciate the love of a partner much greater than I would have before my bleed. This is due to them loving me with my limitations. To love me despite my concerns of mobility, balance and vision, is greater than loving me without these concerns.

Children? How do I feel towards this topic? Did I ever want children? Can I still have children? Well, in all honesty, I was never one for wanting children. Maybe it comes down to never meeting the right guy I would want children with. I don't feel deprived of not having children, and when I look to my future now, it's so knotted up with me and my recovery that there is no space for children. I have to concentrate on myself. How would I carry my child when I don't have a great balance? How would I go out with a pram when my walking isn't great? How am I to feed my child when my vision is damaged? So many questions with the answer, 'can't'. However, I'm at peace with this. As I previously stated, I'm not maternal in any way. I think if I wanted children, I could. I don't think suffering a brain haemorrhage stops you from having children. But I'd have to be quick about it as my age isn't on my side.

The strain this incident has had on my parents is immense. When I first came home in August 2017, I was raw in being a completely different person alongside having no physical stability; I was a floppy mess. My parents had lost their daughter. I was hard; I was cold, spoke my mind, and had no filters. Basically, I was the complete opposite of who I was. Over the years, this new me in personality lessened, though it never entirely disappeared. We are a tight unit, me and my parents, and as hard as it was for them, we did our best; they did their best in supporting me. What happened to me put a strain on our relationship and their relationship with each other. But our love for one another held us together.

My future definitely looks different, and it's one hundred per cent not what I dreamt of; over the current years, I have slightly worried about how I'm expected to live a fulfilling life. I have always wanted to regain my independence, though, at seven years post-bleed, I see that it is looking doubtful. So, I've had to learn to accept this new me. It's the only way I can move forward. I've had to accept that my abilities have now altered. I have to forget what I could do and concentrate on what I can do. I have to focus on what I have gained in my life and the people who stand by my side. I have more genuine loyal friends now than I had before my bleed. My future outlook is different regarding career, house, relationship, travel, etc., but I'm determined to achieve as much of it as possible in my new approach to life. Being complete with yourself helps you live life.

I have recently accepted and given in to getting a mobility scooter. I can't see myself driving anytime soon, and I can't take myself off for a walk. My best option for getting outside is to use a mobility scooter. I never dreamt I'd have one of these, though it's been one of my better decisions. I can now take myself about town; I cannot walk about once there but feel like I am part of society. I can take myself off to look at the beach and sea. It's my freedom, my independence. Having a mobility scooter put me back into society; this would be my new way forward. I've had to swap having a car for a mobility scooter.

This year, 2024, saw me at my worst for my energy levels. I was exhausted; I was tired, and my body hurt. I had to withdraw from all activities slowly, including socialising. I had no strength to participate in the day. My doctor diagnosed me with Chronic Fatigue Syndrome (CFS). I had to prioritise my weekly events and cut down on all I was doing. I had to pace myself. It felt like all the years of trying to improve myself had caught up. This was my realisation that I was no longer strong. Alongside this, I referred myself to talking therapies, which is a type of counselling. This allowed me to express all my troubles. I hadn't cried since the day of the bleed, and I felt that I'd locked my emotions in a box somewhere within my brain. If I could find them and release them, it might help with my energy. I didn't find them, but just talking helped lift the weight of the trauma I was carrying. The counsellor also concluded that I was grieving the old me. This made perfect sense. It was a fault of mine to always compare myself to the old me and feel bad that I could once be able to achieve the task in action.

Question:

What do you miss the most?

I miss my independence the most. Being able to go for a walk has had a huge impact on me, as I now realise just how independent I was. I miss crying. Strange, I know, but I do miss being upset. I also miss driving and being able to take myself off on an adventure. My taste buds changed when I suffered a brain haemorrhage. I no longer taste sweet, and I miss this. I feel I'm missing out on food sensations.

I miss not having a partner, someone with whom to build a future. I'm not saying this is unachievable, but it is somewhat challenging to find. I miss being able to go up and down steps without using a handrail.

Question:

And what do you feel grateful to leave behind from your old life?

What I do like is that my emotions have hardened. I'm no longer soft, and this has made me worry less. I also like the friendships I have formed.

Question:

What would you advise others regarding their future?

I'd advise others in unfortunate health situations to be themselves. Accept your new self because once you accept it, your world opens up. Recovery is a long journey, but with the right people by your side, it can be enjoyable.

"I think the people who have experienced the greatest sadness are the ones who always put the hardest effort to make others happy, because they know in their flesh what it feels like to feel desolate and down and they don't want anyone else to feel that way."

Robin Williams

Chapter Thirteen | Patience

I was just into my seventh-year post-bleed, and I decided to draw a line towards my recovery journey writing. It concludes all the evidence of my slow recovery, which I have shared; recovery does happen, but like anything, it's the time and effort you place into it. At times, you must be the one who asks questions, as the suggestions that you are thinking about and seeking are not always offered to you. I did a lot of research into my recovery to understand the topic of the area I was questioning. You have seen from my account the slow process for which the cogs turn. Sometimes it feels like you have stepped forward and then it is reversed. My brain repair offered a lot of false hope. To this date, August 2024, which is just over seven years from the day of the bleed, recovery is still taking place. Yes, it has slowed down, but it hasn't stopped. I'm still seeking answers to many symptoms, though maybe there are no answers. Being human, it's only natural to seek answers to concerns and symptoms; it keeps the brain active, and we don't like to accept a problem without explanation.

This occurrence has slowed me down somewhat in my actions; I take longer to achieve the simplest of tasks. Some days it's even a mission for me to put my coat on. You are not alone if faced with this. Our brains are no longer natural programmers, post-bleed.

Tiredness is a common symptom post-bleed from reading many articles and forums. When reading my account, you will notice I often document tiredness as an inconvenience.

I've also come to conclude some people will never understand the disabling effect brain injury has on someone. Just because someone sees you not doing something or participating in something doesn't mean the individual is being lazy. Emotions could be screaming out inside that individual to participate, but because they cannot participate, the able-bodied party will give a hard time to the injured individual, sometimes trying to be funny and making light of the situation, only they are causing more emotional damage, making the individual feel worse about themselves.

Through my post-bleed experience with symptoms, I've noted that there are many sensations experienced, and they do fade away, but on occasion, they do reappear. It's a constant battle with finding answers and solutions to these situations.

As I started off with my book, this account you have just read is only my experience. We are all different in our healing journeys. I hope you find comfort and appreciation within my documented experience, which you can relate to if you have also suffered a similar experience.

"Being an inspiration to others would be rewarding."

Jo Ulczak

Thank you

I would like to end my book by saying a big thank you to the following people for staying there for me despite my cognitive and physical changes:

Firstly, my parents, brother and Neil, who have been my immediate support, and then I would like to shout out to my close friends, which include Sarah, James and Emma, my friend from my recovery journey, Annabelle, who's been an amazing inspiration. I am deeply grateful for their unwavering support and understanding during my recovery.

I also want to acknowledge the groups which I have joined and been accepted into with my limited capabilities and mobility - you know who you are. These groups of people are amazing and very accepting of the person you are.

Also, thank you to Sam for believing in me with my writing; with her guidance, I have achieved my book.

Connect With Me

If you've been inspired by my book, please head over to Amazon and leave me a review.

And should you wish to connect, please find me here on Facebook: https://shorturl.at/WlHbC

Or you can email me here: Smile-247@outlook.com

Thank you - Jo x

Printed in Great Britain
by Amazon

58173824R00155